ALL ABOUT
VEGETARIAN COOKING

ALL ABOUT
VEGETARIAN COOKING

IRMA S. ROMBAUER
MARION ROMBAUER BECKER
ETHAN BECKER

PHOTOGRAPHY BY TUCKER & HOSSLER

SCRIBNER
NEW YORK · LONDON · TORONTO · SYDNEY · SINGAPORE

SCRIBNER
1230 Avenue of the Americas
New York, NY 10020

SCRIBNER and design are trademarks of
Macmillan Library Reference USA, Inc.,
used under license by Simon & Schuster,
the publisher of this work.

JOY OF COOKING is a registered trademark
of The Joy of Cooking Trust and
The MRB Revocable Trust.

WELDON OWEN INC.
Chief Executive Officer: John Owen
President: Terry Newell
Chief Operating Officer: Larry Partington
Vice President, International Sales: Stuart Laurence
Publisher: Roger Shaw
Creative Director: Gaye Allen
Associate Publisher: Val Cipollone
Art Director: Jamie Leighton
Production Director: Stephanie Sherman
Designer: Crystal Guertin
Consulting Editors: Judith Dunham, Norman Kolpas
Assistant Editor: Anna Mantzaris
Studio Manager: Brynn Breuner
Pre-press Coordinator: Mario Amador
Production Manager: Chris Hemesath
Food Stylist: Jeff Tucker
Prop Stylist: Sara Slavin
Food Styling Assistants: Rebecca Broder, Angela Kearney
Step-by-Step Photographer: Chris Shorten
Step-by-Step Food Stylist: Kim Brent

Joy of Cooking All About series was designed
and produced by Weldon Owen Inc.,
814 Montgomery Street, San Francisco,
California 94133

Set in Joanna MT and Gill Sans

Separations by Bright Arts Singapore
Printed in Singapore by Tien Wah Press (Pte.) Ltd.

10 9 8 7 6 5 4 3 2 1

Library of Congress Cataloging-in-Publication Data
is available.

ISBN 0-7432-0209-0

Recipe shown on half-title page: *Grilled Eggplant and Roasted Red Pepper Panini*, 42
Recipe shown on title page: *Tart Greens with Apples, Pecans, and Buttermilk Honey Dressing*, 29

CONTENTS

FOREWORD

"To live we must eat. To live in health, we must eat intelligently," wrote my Granny Rom and my mother in the 1962 edition of the Joy of Cooking. More and more people today, for reasons of nutrition, ethics, or faith, choose to live in health by eating a vegetarian diet.

That is why an entire volume in the new All About series is devoted to vegetarian cooking. It offers tips for planning vegetarian meals, information on key ingredients, and recipes for basic beans and grains, stocks, and sauces— everything you need whether you're cooking for a casual luncheon or a special-occasion feast.

You might notice that this collection of kitchen-tested recipes is adapted from the latest edition of the Joy of Cooking. Just as our family has done for generations, we have worked to make this version of Joy a little bit better than the last. As a result, you'll find that some notes, recipes, and techniques have been changed to improve their clarity and usefulness. Since 1931, the Joy of Cooking has constantly evolved. And now, the All About series has taken Joy to a whole new stage, as you will see from the beautiful color photographs of finished dishes and clearly illustrated instructions for preparing and serving them. Granny Rom and Mother would have been delighted.

I'm sure you'll find All About Vegetarian Cooking to be both a useful and an enduring companion in your kitchen.

Enjoy!

Ethan Becker pictured with his grandmother, Irma von Starkloff Rombauer (left), and his mother, Marion Rombauer Becker (right). Irma Rombauer published the first Joy of Cooking at her own expense in 1931. Marion Rombauer Becker became coauthor in 1951. Joy as it has progressed through the decades (from top left to bottom right): the 1931 edition with Marion's depiction of St. Martha of Bethany, said to be the patron saint of cooking, "slaying the dragon of kitchen drudgery"; the 1943 edition; the 1951 edition; the 1962 edition; the 1975 edition; and the 1997 edition.

About Vegetarian Cooking

So many people call themselves vegetarians these days that it's easy to fall into the mistaken belief that all vegetarians are alike. Such a simplistic point of view couldn't be further from the truth, and it gets in the way of understanding the many facets of vegetarian cooking and important related nutritional issues.

Vegetarians choose to be so for a wide variety of reasons. Many of the world's populations, such as the Hindus of India, follow vegetarian diets for religious reasons. Others follow near-vegetarian diets mandated by the scarcity of meat and other animal products in certain areas. Some people opt for a vegetarian diet as a consequence of ethical beliefs about animal rights. Growing numbers shun animal products for environmental reasons, claiming that growing plants is more ecologically efficient and responsible than raising livestock. Still others shift to a vegetarian diet to take advantage of the generally low-fat, cholesterol-free, high-fiber, and nutrient-rich nature of plant foods.

Specific types of vegetarian diets vary as much as the reasons for choosing them. The major approaches are:

Lacto-vegetarian: Includes dairy products along with vegetables, fruits, and grains, but eliminates eggs.

Ovo-vegetarian: Includes eggs along with vegetables, fruits, and grains, but eliminates dairy products.

Lacto-ovo vegetarian: Includes dairy products and eggs along with vegetables, fruits, and grains.

Macrobiotic: Emphasizes cooked foods, especially whole grains, with moderate amounts of vegetables and beans, minimal fruits, little if any dairy foods or eggs, and occasional small servings of mild white fish.

Vegan: Rules out all animal products, including such staples as eggs and cheese, concentrating solely on vegetables, legumes, fruits, and grains.

In addition, many people today may call themselves vegetarians while still including seafood in their diets. Or they may cut out only red meat, but eat both fish and poultry, or may indulge from time to time in poultry or meat, or even enjoy meals in which plant foods predominate but which may occasionally include very small amounts of animal protein. Such habits clearly push the envelope on the definition of "vegetarian." But vegetarians of all persuasions and preferences will find a bounty of useful and appealing recipes on the pages that follow. So, too, will those who want to add a greater variety of plant foods to their diets.

BUYING LOCALLY

Foods grown locally, most commonly found at the farmers' markets, do not require long-distance transportation and therefore do not contribute as greatly to pollution as items shipped long distances. Small local farmers are also more adventurous in the variety of produce they grow, often offering heirloom vegetables and fruits with dazzling colors, patterns, shapes, tastes, and textures. They are also more likely to follow organic farming methods. Locally produced foods, organic or not, tend to be fresher and thus more flavorful and nutritious.

Organic Ingredients

Strong adherents to the philosophy that you are what you eat, many vegetarians seek out organic ingredients, and with good reason. Pesticides, insecticides, herbicides, and fungicides are widely used in agriculture worldwide to protect food crops from worms, insects, weeds, or fungi that may affect their quality and their profitability. Most of the produce we buy in the supermarket—virtually everything that isn't labeled "organic"—has been grown with one or more of these agents. Therefore, careful buying of ingredients and cleaning of produce are clearly important.

Whether or not you are a strict vegetarian, you should try, whenever possible, to buy organic products and other ingredients. Until recently, however, it has been difficult in many states for consumers to be sure that the foods they are purchasing are indeed organic.

In early 2000, the National Organic Program of the U.S. Department of Agriculture (USDA) approved a set of national standards that regulates the growing and production of organic foods and their labeling. Intended for national use, this program applies to both fresh produce and processed foods made with organic ingredients. Only certified products that are at least 95 percent organic and meet other criteria are permitted to carry the USDA seal. As the popularity of buying organic foods grows, this uniform labeling will help consumers make informed and more reliable choices.

Although foods labeled organic are grown without the use of pesticides and their relatives, this does not guarantee that organic foods are 100 percent free of harmful chemicals, residuals of which may come from rainwater, irrigation water, or the soil. Nor do tests show that organic foods are necessarily higher in nutrients or flavor. Buying such products, however, increases your odds of getting safer, better-quality, better-tasting ingredients than those that are mass-produced.

Just as important is supporting small-scale community-based farms. More and more today, agriculture is concentrated in the hands of large corporations, a trend supported by governments through water and land subsidies and tax abatements. As a result, we are now able to buy almost any kind of "seasonal" food the year around, and often at very low prices. But there are hidden costs: the impact of the overuse of fertilizers and pesticides on the quality of our land, water, and air; the despoiling of tropical forests and jungles to produce meat and winter vegetables; and the damage done to the birds, frogs, pollinating insects, and other creatures with which we share our ecosystem.

Pay attention to proposed legislative changes affecting food labeling, food safety, agricultural production, and the quality of our land, air, and water, and let your legislators know how you feel about them. The political arena is full of lobbyists representing enterprises that would like to weaken regulations or shift the burden of compliance from industry to understaffed agencies. If we are what we eat, we need to do everything we can to protect our precious food resources.

Nutrition for Vegetarians

Most vegetarians follow healthful diets and as long as calories are adequate and food sources vary, vegetarian diets can provide all essential nutrients and are ample in protein. Vegetarian diets are also appropriate for children as long as they contain enough fats and calories and a sufficient variety of foods to support growth.

Achieving the goal of adequate calories and balanced and varied food sources may present a greater challenge to some vegetarians. Keep *Dietary Essentials, 12*, in mind when planning vegetarian diets. Also, pay close attention to the recommended daily servings on the Food Guide Pyramid (*below left*) developed by the United States Department of Agriculture (USDA) and to that agency's guidelines for serving sizes (*opposite*).

As indicated by the USDA pyramid, food plants clearly constitute the foundation of a healthful diet, and therefore many servings of grains, vegetables, and fruits should be chosen daily by vegetarians and nonvegetarians alike. Vegetarians who eliminate all meat, fish, and poultry from their diets need to substitute other sources of protein, such as additional servings of beans and nuts.

The serving recommendations noted on the pyramid may seem unreasonable—who eats 6 to 11 servings of grain a day? But this is only because the USDA doesn't

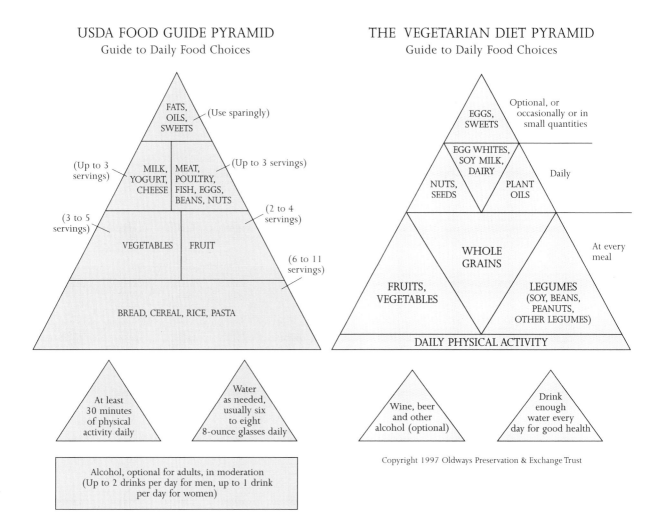

USDA FOOD GUIDE PYRAMID
Guide to Daily Food Choices

FATS, OILS, SWEETS — (Use sparingly)

(Up to 3 servings) — MILK, YOGURT, CHEESE | MEAT, POULTRY, FISH, EGGS, BEANS, NUTS — (Up to 3 servings)

(3 to 5 servings) — VEGETABLES | FRUIT — (2 to 4 servings)

(6 to 11 servings)

BREAD, CEREAL, RICE, PASTA

At least 30 minutes of physical activity daily

Water as needed, usually six to eight 8-ounce glasses daily

Alcohol, optional for adults, in moderation (Up to 2 drinks per day for men, up to 1 drink per day for women)

THE VEGETARIAN DIET PYRAMID
Guide to Daily Food Choices

EGGS, SWEETS — Optional, or occasionally or in small quantities

EGG WHITES, SOY MILK, DAIRY

NUTS, SEEDS | PLANT OILS — Daily

WHOLE GRAINS

FRUITS, VEGETABLES | LEGUMES (SOY, BEANS, PEANUTS, OTHER LEGUMES) — At every meal

DAILY PHYSICAL ACTIVITY

Wine, beer and other alcohol (optional)

Drink enough water every day for good health

use the term *serving* the way most of us do. As the agency defines the term, a 1-inch cube of cheese counts as a serving of dairy; a single serving of cold breakfast cereal (a grain) measures 1 ounce; and a 6-ounce muffin from the corner bakery counts as 6 grain servings, the minimum recommendation for one day.

Not all nutritionists accept the Food Guide Pyramid as gospel. For example, proponents of the so-called Mediterranean diet—based originally on traditional consumption patterns in Greece and southern Italy, where heart disease and related ailments are comparatively rare—argue for a greater amount of fat, in the form of olive oil, cheese, and yogurt, than the USDA would prefer.

To show other healthful ways of eating, Oldways Preservation & Exchange Trust, a nonprofit educational organization based in Cambridge, Massachusetts, has developed alternative pyramids. The one for vegetarians (*opposite right*) was created jointly by Oldways and the Harvard School of Public Health. Among its differences from the USDA pyramid, it places greater emphasis on the importance of all forms of legumes, singles out soy milk as an important part of the dairy group, and recommends less frequent consumption of whole eggs. At the foundation of the vegetarian pyramid, and integral to it, is daily physical activity.

Most of us, though, do not always eat according to pyramids, charts, and government regulations. We don't want to take all the fun out of eating, and indeed we shouldn't. What's important for following a vegetarian diet is to develop sensible eating habits overall, skewing our diet in the right direction. If we eat foods that are chosen according to sensible guidelines and are consumed in sensible amounts, all of the nutritional requirements will be met.

RULES FOR SERVING SIZES*

Protein Group (dried beans, eggs, and nuts)
- 1 to 1½ cups cooked dried beans
- 2 to 3 eggs
- 2 tablespoons peanut butter or ⅓ cup nuts counts as ⅓ to ½ serving

Milk Group (milk, yogurt, and cheese)
- 1 cup milk or yogurt
- 1½ ounces natural cheese
- 2 ounces processed cheese

Grain Products Group (bread, cereal, rice, and pasta)
- 1 slice bread
- 1 ounce ready-to-eat cereal
- ½ cup cooked cereal, rice, or pasta

Vegetable Group
- 1 cup raw leafy vegetables
- ½ cup other vegetables—cooked or raw
- ¾ cup vegetable juice

Fruit Group
- 1 medium apple, banana, or orange
- ½ cup chopped, cooked, or canned fruit
- ¾ cup fruit juice

Alcohol
- 12 ounces regular beer
- 5 ounces wine
- 1.5 ounces 80-proof distilled spirits

* Some foods fit into more than one group. Dried beans, peas, and lentils are "crossover foods" that can be counted as servings in either the protein group or the vegetable group, but not both. Serving sizes indicated here are those used in the Food Guide Pyramid (*opposite left*) and are based on both suggested and usually consumed portions necessary to achieve adequate nutrient intake. They differ from serving sizes on the Nutrition Facts labels of packaged foods, which reflect portions usually consumed.

(Adapted from *The 1995 Dietary Guidelines for Americans,* 4th edition. USDA, USDHHS, HG 232)

Dietary Essentials

Although a varied vegetarian diet should provide all the nutrients you need, it is important to keep a few key nutrients in mind when planning meals.

Protein: Protein is essential for its nitrogen and amino acids, which are the building blocks for muscles, skin, connective tissues, and almost every other body part. The chief components of protein are twenty amino acids that are needed to build tissue properly. Of these twenty, eleven are "nonessential," as your body is able to synthesize them on its own; the remaining nine cannot be synthesized and must be ingested regularly. These nine are known as essential amino acids. Protein from vegetable sources such as whole grains, nuts, seeds, and legumes can satisfy all of your protein needs without meat consumption. However, because any given vegetable source will not provide all essential amino acids, it is important, especially for vegans, to eat a good variety of protein-rich vegetarian foods. Despite a commonly held belief, it is not necessary to combine different sources in the same meal to provide your body with complete proteins.

Iron: Your body needs iron to help build red blood cells and transport oxygen through the bloodstream. The most readily absorbable type of iron, called heme iron, is present in animal proteins. Dairy products, eggs, and plant foods, by contrast, are higher in non-heme iron, only 2 to 20 percent of which is absorbable. That makes it all the more important for vegetarians to consume iron-rich foods such as leafy greens, whole grains, soybeans and tofu, members of the cabbage family, and root vegetables. Eating foods rich in vitamin C, such as citrus fruits, black currants, guavas, berries, broccoli, and bell peppers, will also help increase iron absorption.

Vitamin B$_{12}$: Found only in animal products, this vitamin is essential for maintaining the nervous system and producing red blood cells. Vegetarians who eat dairy products should get sufficient quantities. Vegans, however, should take B$_{12}$ supplements.

Vitamin D: Necessary for your body's absorption of calcium, the formation of teeth and bones, and the functioning of the nervous system and muscles, this vitamin is synthesized by exposure to adequate sunlight. It is also present in commercially sold fortified milk. Particularly during winter months, vegans should take vitamin D supplements.

Energy intake: Very high-fiber diets, more likely to occur for vegetarians than nonvegetarians, can restrict somewhat the body's absorption of nutrients and intake of energy. Vegetarian parents should take special care that their children are getting sufficient nutrients and calories for proper development. So, too, should seniors and pregnant or lactating women.

Planning Vegetarian Menus

Creating menus for your family and guests may seem challenging if you're new to following a vegetarian diet, but after a while, you'll find the process easy and enjoyable. Begin your planning by considering the season, for you will want to use, if possible, produce at its seasonal peak. Also take into account the climate, the time of day, the likes and dislikes of those at the table, and, of course, your nutritional needs.

The following menus are examples of the many meals you can put together using the recipes in this book, substituting dishes to suit your tastes, talents, and time. Countless other combinations can be devised. For a simple lunch or dinner, pair a salad made with fresh greens with a robust vegetable stew or pasta, or offer a hearty main-dish salad on its own. You'll find dishes made with grains, beans, and tofu and plenty of vegetable dishes that can be served with them. Just add your favorite beverage and fresh fruit or other dessert to complete the meal.

MIDDLE EASTERN COCKTAIL PARTY
Hummus, 45
Baba Ghanoush, 45
Zucchini Pancakes with Mint and
    Feta Cheese, 63
Greek Spinach and Cheese Pie, 69

ITALIAN GARDEN LUNCH
Arugula with Summer Vegetables, 28
Grilled Pizza with Tomato and Three
    Cheeses, 48

FAMILY-STYLE SUPPER
Salad with Basic Vinaigrette, 27
Mushroom Ragout, 67
Oven-Baked Polenta, 108

ASIAN FEAST
Vegetarian Wonton Soup, 22
Stir-Fried Bok Choy with
    Mushrooms, 57
Szechuan Spiced Tofu, 87
Fried Rice, 101

SOUP AND SALAD
Deluxe Squash Soup, 21
Tart Greens with Apples, Pecans, and
    Buttermilk Honey Dressing, 29

CASUAL INDIAN BUFFET
Potato and Eggplant Curry with
    Tomato and Fresh Cilantro, 64
Saag Paneer, 64
Curried Chickpeas with
    Vegetables, 84
Basic Pilaf, 103

WARMING WINTER SUPPER
Winter Vegetable Couscous, 112
Harissa, 112

HEARTY BRUNCH
Huevos Rancheros, 119
Refried Beans, 81
Jícama Salad, 32

WEEKNIGHT SUPPER
Smoked Tofu Burgers, 87
Peruvian Potato Salad, 34
Rye Berry Salad with Roasted Pepper
    Dressing, 37

MAKE-AHEAD LUNCH
Artichoke Frittata, 118
Chickpea Salad, 38
Focaccia, 42

ABOUT **STOCKS** & SOUPS

*I*f any food seems inherently calming, and even consoling, it is soup. Soup feels good when the weather gets cold. It restores our spirit and our vigor. (The first "restaurants" were eighteenth-century Parisian establishments that served rich soups to restore, or *restaurer,* the hungry citizenry.) In the old days, when a "soup bunch" of vegetables and herbs cost a nickel, American home cooks routinely made soups from scratch. Today, the smell of soup simmering still symbolizes home cooking.

Soup of Garden Greens with Parmesan Threads, 19

Preparing Stocks

Stocks are a vital ingredient in many sauces, soups, and other foods, and no store-bought variety can compare with a well-tended homemade version. Stock making is different from other kinds of cooking. Instead of calling for tender, young ingredients, stocks are best made with mature vegetables, cooked slowly for a long time to extract every vestige of flavor.

The characteristics of any good stock are flavor, body, and clarity. Of the three, flavor is paramount, and the way to get it is by using a high proportion of ingredients to water. The most flavorful stocks are made with only enough water to cover the vegetables. Additional water is needed only when the liquid evaporates below the level of the ingredients before the stock is fully cooked. Follow the stock recipes for ideal ratios of liquid to solids, but the principle is simple: Keep the solids covered while cooking.

Vegetable stocks rarely require more than an hour to cook. In fact, their delicate flavors deteriorate if overcooked. When preparing ingredients for stock making, it is important to chop vegetables to size according to their cooking times—large for long cooking and small for quick cooking—to allow their flavors to be fully extracted.

HOW TO STRAIN AND STORE STOCK

It is easy to strain and store your own stock at home. When the stock is chilled, any fat will rise in a solid mass that must be removed before reheating. While cold, this fat layer actually protects the stock.

1 When the stock has finished cooking, strain it through a fine-mesh sieve (or a colander lined with a double layer of cheese-cloth or a coffee filter) into another pot or a large heatproof container and discard the solids. We recommend pressing heavily on the solids while straining for the vegetable stock recipes, where the extra flavor from the cooked vegetables is needed. Do not let the stock sit out at room temperature for long as it is a good breeding ground for bacteria.

2 Speed up the cooling process by placing the hot pot, uncovered, in a sink or bowl of ice water and stirring it a few times. Once the stock cools enough so that it will not raise the temperature of your refrigerator, cover it tightly and chill it.

3 Stock will keep for 3 to 5 days in the refrigerator. If refrigerated for longer, boil the stock for 10 minutes, then refrigerate it for another 3 to 5 days. For prolonged storage, transfer stock to pint or quart plastic containers or plastic freezer bags and freeze it. Small amounts of stock can also be frozen in ice cube trays.

Vegetable Stock

About 4 cups

Beyond the standard recipe here, vegetable stocks allow for much improvisation. Good additions include potatoes, corncobs, fennel, ginger, washed organic vegetable skins, and even a few tablespoons of lentils. A small amount of soy sauce and a pinch of red pepper flakes can also be added. Vegetables to avoid include those in the cabbage family (except when used deliberately and with discretion), eggplant, and most strong greens (with the exception of kale); too many carrots or parsnips will turn the stock overly sweet (we like to include a small turnip to add complexity to the stock and to offset the sweetness of the carrot). When possible, tailor the ingredients to suit the recipe the stock will be used in. For example, a stock accented with ginger and garlic would be good in many Asian recipes. In general, 5 cups vegetables to 6 cups water makes about 3 to 4 cups stock.

Combine in a stockpot:

1 medium onion, sliced
1 leek, white part only, cleaned thoroughly and sliced
1 carrot, peeled and sliced
1 small turnip, peeled and sliced
6 cloves garlic, peeled and smashed
6 cups cold water
1 Bouquet Garni, right

Simmer gently, partially covered, until the vegetables are completely softened, 45 to 60 minutes. Strain into a clean pot or heatproof plastic container, pressing down on the vegetables to extract the juices.

Season with:

Salt and ground black pepper to taste (optional)

Let cool, uncovered, then refrigerate until ready to use.

Roasted Vegetable Stock

About 4 cups

Preheat the oven to 400°F. Lightly grease a roasting pan.

Toss together in the prepared pan and roast, stirring occasionally, until well browned, about 1 hour:

8 ounces mushrooms or mushroom stems, wiped clean
1 onion, quartered
2 carrots, peeled and cut into 2-inch pieces
8 cloves garlic, peeled and smashed
1 small turnip, peeled and cut into 2-inch pieces

Remove the vegetables to a stockpot, then deglaze the hot roasting pan by adding:

1 cup cold water

Scrape up any browned bits, then add the liquid to the pot along with:

6 cups cold water
1 Bouquet Garni, right, including a pinch of red pepper flakes

Simmer gently, uncovered, until the vegetables are completely softened, 45 to 60 minutes. Strain into a clean pot or heatproof plastic container, pressing down on the vegetables to extract the juices. Season with:

Salt to taste

Let cool, uncovered, then refrigerate until ready to use.

Bouquet Garni

Since herbs tend to float, we recommend tying them together in a little packet, known as a bouquet garni. Vary the contents to suit your dish, with additions such as whole cloves, dill, lemon zest, or garlic. For express broth or quick-cooking stocks, there is no need to tie the seasonings in a bundle—they can simply be tossed in with the vegetables.

Wrap in a 4 x 4-inch piece of cheesecloth:

Small bunch of parsley or parsley stems
8 sprigs fresh thyme, or 1 teaspoon dried
1 bay leaf
2 or 3 celery leaves (optional)

Tie the cheesecloth securely with a piece of kitchen string or omit the cheesecloth and simply tie the herbs together at their stems. Refrigerate in a tightly covered container until ready to use.

Cajun Black-Eyed Pea Soup

About 8 cups

The Louisiana culinary trinity—onions, peppers, and celery—flavors this hearty country soup.

Rinse, sort, and soak, 78:

1 pound (about 2½ cups) dried black-eyed peas

In a soup pot, gently cook, covered, but stirring occasionally, until tender, but not brown:

3 medium stalks celery, diced (about 1½ cups)

2 medium onions, diced (about 2 cups)

1 medium green bell pepper, diced (about 1 cup)

1 medium red bell pepper, diced (about 1 cup)

2 cloves garlic, minced

3 tablespoons vegetable oil

Drain and add the black-eyed peas along with:

10 cups cold water

Simmer, partially covered, until the beans are tender, about 1 hour. Using a potato masher, mash just enough beans in the pot to slightly thicken the soup. Season with:

2 tablespoons Worcestershire sauce

2 to 3 teaspoons hot red pepper sauce, or to taste

1 tablespoon salt

Ladle into warmed bowls. Garnish with:

Sliced scallion greens

BLACK-EYED PEAS

Black-eyed peas are members of the mung bean family. They have a fuller vegetable flavor than most beans. A small black dot, which remains visible after cooking, names the cream-colored beans, which are also known as black-eye Susans and are very closely related to yellow-eye and crowder peas. If you wish to substitute fresh or frozen black-eyed peas for dried, use triple the cup amount called for and cook just until the beans are tender, 15 to 30 minutes, depending on the maturity and whether they are frozen.

Broccoli Cheddar Soup

About 6 cups

This is a good soup to add to your permanent repertoire. It can be made quickly with ingredients often at hand, and it solves the problem of what to make for dinner when accompanied by a big salad and a loaf of good bread.

In a soup pot, melt over medium-low heat:

3 tablespoons unsalted butter or vegetable oil

Add:

1 cup chopped onions, or leeks, cleaned thoroughly
½ cup chopped celery
4 cups broccoli florets, coarsely chopped

Cook, stirring, until tender, about 5 minutes. Sprinkle over the top:

⅓ cup all-purpose flour

Stir well to blend, increase the heat to medium, and cook, stirring constantly, for 5 minutes. (Make sure not to burn the flour.) Gradually add and stir until smooth:

4 cups *Vegetable Stock*, 17
2 cups milk

Cook until the vegetables are tender, about 5 minutes more. Transfer to a food processor and puree until smooth. Return the soup to the pot and return to a low simmer. Stir in in batches, blending well after each addition:

2 cups grated Cheddar cheese

Be very careful not to boil this soup: If the soup is too hot the cheese will break down. Season with:

1 tablespoon Dijon mustard
¼ teaspoon ground black pepper
Salt to taste
Hot red pepper sauce to taste (optional)
Worcestershire sauce to taste (optional)

Garnish the soup with:

Grated Cheddar cheese

Soup of Garden Greens with Parmesan Threads

About 10 cups

Fresh herbs bring vibrance, while a good Parmesan cheese lends an appealing nuttiness to this quick vegetable soup. Add and subtract vegetables depending on what the garden and market yield. Serve with a whole-grain bread.

In a large soup pot, cook, stirring, over medium-low heat until wilted, about 10 minutes:

2 medium carrots, peeled and finely diced (about 1½ cups)
2 medium zucchini, finely diced (about 2½ cups)
2 large onions, finely diced (about 3 cups)

in:

2 tablespoons extra-virgin olive oil

Add:

8 to 10 cups *Vegetable Stock*, 17

If not using fresh herbs at the end, add:

2 teaspoons dried basil

½ teaspoon dried oregano

Boil, partially covered, until the vegetables are tender, about 10 minutes. Meanwhile beat together and set aside:

2 large eggs
1 cup freshly grated Parmesan (about 8 ounces)

Drop into the soup and simmer, uncovered, 1 minute:

6 large romaine or escarole leaves, shredded
⅓ cup packed fresh basil, minced
⅓ cup packed fresh parsley, minced
1 tablespoon packed fresh oregano, chopped

Remove the soup from the heat and whisk in the egg mixture, stirring slowly so that it forms thin, firm threads. Season to taste with:

Salt and ground black pepper

Serve hot.

PARMIGIANO-REGGIANO

This mouth-filling cow's milk cheese with a complex and pleasing aftertaste is made in a small, legally designated area of Emilia-Romagna in northern Italy. It is the only true Parmesan. All the others are imitations. Remember that older is not better. Today's Parmigiano-Reggiano usually reaches its peak at about two years. Before World War II, when different cows gave Parmigiano-Reggiano milk, the cheese successfully aged longer. A dry Jack and a Wisconsin Asiago are closer in flavor than American and Argentinian Parmesans. Grated Parmigiano-Reggiano is a wonderful addition to soups. This cheese is also excellent simply picked up in the fingers and nibbled after informal Italian meals.

Spinach Soup

About 5 cups

In a soup pot, cook, stirring, over medium-low heat until tender but not brown:

¼ cup minced onion
2 cloves garlic, minced

in:

2 tablespoons unsalted butter

Stir in:

2 tablespoons all-purpose flour

Cook, stirring constantly, over medium heat for 5 minutes. Do not brown the flour. Gradually whisk in:

4 cups milk

Simmer, stirring occasionally, over low heat, until slightly thickened, about 10 minutes. Meanwhile bring a large pot of water to a boil. Stem and wash thoroughly:

1 pound spinach

Plunge the spinach leaves in the boiling water for 1 minute. Immediately drain and rinse with cold water. Puree until smooth. Add half the soup to the spinach and continue to process until smooth. Stir the puree into the remaining soup (*opposite*).

Season with:

1 teaspoon salt
¼ teaspoon freshly grated or ground nutmeg
¼ teaspoon ground black pepper

Escarole, Garlic, and Tomato Soup

About 5 cups

In a soup pot, cook, stirring, over medium-low heat, until tender but not brown:

1 medium onion, chopped (about 1 cup)
5 cloves garlic, minced

in:

3 tablespoons olive oil or other vegetable oil

Add:

2 medium, ripe tomatoes, peeled, seeded, chopped, with their juices reserved (about 2 cups)
3 cups *Vegetable Stock*, 17

Bring to a boil. Reduce the heat and simmer, uncovered, 5 minutes. Add:

4 cups tightly packed coarsely chopped escarole (1 small head)
1 teaspoon salt
¼ to ½ teaspoon ground black pepper

Simmer, uncovered, until the escarole is softened, about 5 minutes. Ladle into warmed bowls. Garnish with:

Chopped fresh basil or *Pesto Sauce*, 96 (optional)

Deluxe Squash Soup

About 6 cups

Preheat the oven to 400°F. Place on a large baking sheet:

1 large butternut squash

Drizzle over the top:

2 tablespoons olive oil

Roast for 45 minutes. Cover the squash with aluminum foil and roast until tender, about 15 more minutes. When cool enough to handle, scrape the pulp from the skin into a food processor and pour in the pan juices. Add and puree until smooth:

1 cup *Vegetable Stock*, 17

In a large saucepan, heat over medium-low heat:

2 tablespoons olive oil

Add and cook, stirring, until tender but not brown, about 5 minutes:

1 small onion, minced (about ½ cup)
1 small carrot, minced (about ½ cup)
1 stalk celery, finely chopped (about ⅓ cup)

Add the pureed squash along with:

¼ teaspoon ground cinnamon
¼ teaspoon ground nutmeg
¼ teaspoon ground ginger

Add:

4 cups *Vegetable Stock*, 17

Bring to a boil, reduce the heat to medium, and simmer, stirring from time to time, until the vegetables are tender, about 10 minutes. Stir in:

½ cup heavy cream

Season to taste with:

Salt and ground black pepper

Divide among 6 soup bowls:

1 cup cooked wild rice (about ½ cup uncooked)

Ladle the soup over rice and serve.

Vegetarian Wonton Soup

6 to 8 servings; 6 cups soup and about 30 wontons

Homemade wontons are easy to prepare with readily available premade wrappers. When cooking wontons, keep the water at a low simmer to prevent them from opening. Fresh or dried mushrooms can be used in this filling.

Either soak for 30 minutes:

6 dried medium shiitake mushrooms (optional)

in:

2 cups hot water

Drain the mushrooms, straining the soaking liquid through a fine-mesh sieve lined with a dampened paper towel. Remove the mushroom stems, and thinly slice.

Or thinly slice:

8 fresh shiitake mushrooms (about 1½ cups sliced)

In a large skillet, heat over medium heat:

1 tablespoon vegetable oil

Add the shiitake mushrooms along with:

2 cups chopped white mushrooms (about 5 ounces)

8 ounces firm tofu, drained and crumbled (about 1½ cups)

2 scallions, chopped (about ½ cup)

½ cup thinly sliced Napa cabbage

1 tablespoon minced fresh ginger

Sauté until the vegetables are wilted, about 5 minutes.

Let cool, then season with:

2 tablespoons light or dark soy sauce

1 tablespoon toasted sesame oil

1 tablespoon dry sherry or Shaoxing wine

1 teaspoon chili oil (optional)

1 teaspoon sugar

½ teaspoon salt

⅛ teaspoon ground black pepper

In a small bowl, stir together:

1 large egg

1 tablespoon water

Working in batches of 10 at a time, lay out the first batch of:

Wonton wrappers

To assemble, arrange wrappers so that one point is facing you, in a diamond pattern. Lightly brush each wrapper with the egg wash. Place a teaspoon of filling in the center of each wrapper. Fold the wonton in half, by bringing the top corner to meet the bottom corner, forming a triangle. Seal by pressing the edges firmly, squeezing all the air out as you seal. To finish, bring the two outside corners to meet at the center and press to seal. If the wonton wrappers start to dry out, moisten the corners with egg wash. When all the wontons are assembled, set aside.

In a soup pot, bring to a simmer:

5 cups *Vegetable Stock*, 17, or 1 cup reserved mushroom-soaking liquid and 4 cups *Vegetable Stock*

Season with:

1⅛ teaspoons salt

Cover and keep warm.

Bring a large pot of water to a simmer. Drop in the wontons in 2 or 3 batches and simmer gently until done, about 5 minutes. Drain, then divide among individual bowls. Ladle the hot broth over the wontons.

Garnish with:

Decoratively cut carrots

Chopped scallion greens

ABOUT
SALADS

*A*lthough the term salad once meant nothing more than lettuce tossed with oil and vinegar, today's salads are made from almost every sort of vegetable, pasta, grain, or legume, raw or cooked, cold or warm, tied together by a flavorful dressing. Every step in creating a salad, from selecting ingredients to serving it, allows for the cook's imagination to play its part.

A simple green salad is an excellent way to refresh the palate after the main course of a large dinner and a perfect preparation for the dessert to come. A plate of marinated vegetables will spark the appetite before the main course. Salads can also replace vegetable side dishes. And finally, there are more and more instances where salad becomes the entire meal.

Tart Greens with Apples, Pecans, and Buttermilk Honey Dressing, 29

Preparing Greens for Salads

Buy the freshest greens with crisp leaves, free of brown spots on leaves or stems. Greens still attached to their roots are usually more intense in flavor than those severed at the stem. Use greens as soon as possible after buying them. If you have to store them, remove any leaves that are wilted or show signs of decay and take off any rubber or metal bands holding greens together. Unwashed greens will keep for 3 to 4 days at most. Store greens in the vegetable bin of your refrigerator in a plastic bag with holes poked in it. Properly washing, drying, and chilling salad greens is the indispensable first step in any salad.

Always handle greens carefully, so as not to bruise them. The easiest way to wash them is to separate the leaves and place them in a large bowl or sink full of cold water, swish them around for 30 seconds

or so, then lift them from the water gently so that the dirt and grit remain in the water. Repeat the process until the water is clear.

For drying, salad spinners are a wonderful convenience. Overcrowding a salad spinner, however, will both bruise the greens and hinder the device's ability to dry them adequately. A spinner about one-half to two-thirds full will work perfectly every time. Alternatively, dry greens by tossing lightly in a colander, tapping your fingers against the underside of the colander to make sure all the water runs out. In either case, it will probably be necessary to wrap them in absorbent paper towels for the final drying. Whatever the method, once dried, the greens should be well chilled to render them crisp. Tear or cut them only when you are about to make the salad.

Garnishing Green Salads

A green salad is easily transformed into a main course with the addition of a few ingredients chosen for texture, taste, and visual appeal. The greens remain dominant in these salads, so avoid the temptation to overwhelm them with too many bits of this and that. Think in terms of balance and harmony. Too many assertive garnishes will cancel each other out. On the other hand, too many sweet flavors—fruit, soft cheese, carrots, and tomatoes—may become cloying. Begin by tasting the greens. If they are strong and pungent, they can support more flavor; mild and

tender greens tolerate less. The simplest way to enhance a green salad is to add condiments or seasonings to the salad while or after you toss it with the dressing. Be sure to give the greens a few extra tosses to integrate the additions well. With a light coat of dressing on the greens, small accents such as croutons, nuts, cheese, and olives will cling to the salad and are less apt to fall to the bottom of the bowl. For more substantial additions like the multiple ingredients of a Greek salad, everything gets tossed together at once.

Dressing Salads

The time to dress green salads is always at the very last minute. Once dressed, greens become limp if they sit too long. Place the greens in a bowl large enough to hold them spaciously. Pour the dressing or its ingredients down the side to form a puddle at the bottom. The tossing can now be done with clean hands, a pair of tongs, a couple of ordinary wooden kitchen spoons, or the over-sized fork and spoon known as a salad set. Reach into the bottom of the bowl and gently lift the greens so that the topmost greens fall to the bottom. Gently repeat this action until all the dressing is distributed.

MAKING A VINAIGRETTE

The most surefire way to make a thick, well-emulsified vinaigrette is to first whisk together the vinegar or lemon juice and the seasonings (salt, minced shallots or other members of the onion tribe, and mustard) in a small bowl. Then slowly add the oil, drop by drop, whisking as you go, until the dressing begins to thicken. Add the oil in more of a steady stream as the dressing becomes noticeably thicker.

An alternative, and perhaps more convenient, technique is to place the vinegar or lemon juice and seasonings in a small jar with a tight-fitting lid and shake to blend. Then add the oil in three or four additions, shaking vigorously between additions. A third and equally popular method is to mix the vinegar and seasonings in a blender and then add the oil in a slow, steady stream with the machine running. Vinaigrette can be stored, tightly covered, in the refrigerator for up to 2 weeks. Always whisk dressings briskly just before adding them to salads so that the ingredients are well mixed and in balance, and don't add more vinaigrette than is necessary to lightly coat the salad.

Basic Vinaigrette

About 1 ½ cups

The optional ingredients help maintain the emulsion of oil and vinegar.
If garlic flavor is desired, mash together until a paste is formed:

1 small clove garlic, peeled
2 to 3 pinches of salt

Remove to a small bowl or a jar with a tight-fitting lid. Add and whisk or shake until well blended:

⅓ to ½ cup red wine vinegar or
    fresh lemon juice
1 shallot, minced
1 teaspoon Dijon mustard
    (optional)
Salt and ground black pepper
    to taste

Add in a slow, steady stream, whisking constantly, or add to the jar and shake until smooth:

1 cup extra-virgin olive oil

Taste and adjust the seasonings. Use at once or cover and refrigerate.

FRESH HERB VINAIGRETTE

Prepare *Basic Vinaigrette, left,* adding ⅓ cup minced or finely snipped fresh herbs (basil, dill, parsley, chives, and/or thyme).

LEMON CAPER VINAIGRETTE

Prepare *Basic Vinaigrette, left,* with fresh lemon juice and add 1 tablespoon minced drained capers, 1 tablespoon minced fresh parsley, and ½ teaspoon finely grated lemon zest.

BASIL CHIVE VINAIGRETTE

Prepare *Basic Vinaigrette, left,* adding ⅓ cup minced fresh basil, ⅓ cup finely snipped fresh chives, and, if desired, 1 tablespoon walnut oil.

GREEN PEPPERCORN VINAIGRETTE

Prepare *Basic Vinaigrette, left,* adding 2 tablespoons minced drained green peppercorns or 1 tablespoon cracked dried green peppercorns.

LIME VINAIGRETTE

Prepare *Basic Vinaigrette, left,* substituting ¼ cup fresh lime juice for the vinegar or lemon juice and, if desired, adding a large pinch of toasted cumin seeds.

BLACK PEPPER VINAIGRETTE

Prepare *Basic Vinaigrette, left,* adding 1 teaspoon finely grated lemon zest and 2 teaspoons cracked black peppercorns, or to taste.

Arugula with Summer Vegetables

4 to 6 servings

Use this recipe as a rough guideline, substituting whatever summer vegetables are most plentiful in the market. Baby turnip or beet greens or Swiss chard leaves can be substituted for the arugula.

Prepare:

Basic Vinaigrette, 27, or one of the variations

Cook in a large pot of boiling water for about 1 minute:

1 small summer squash, cut into ½-inch cubes, or 6 pattypan squash, cut in half

Remove with a large slotted spoon, refresh in ice water, and drain well. Add to the boiling water:

8 ounces thin green beans, trimmed

Cook just until crisp-tender, about 1 minute. Remove with a large slotted spoon, refresh in ice water, and drain well. Combine the squash and green beans in a salad bowl along with:

2 cups cherry tomatoes, halved

1 small red onion, halved and very thinly sliced

⅓ cup minced fresh basil

Toss well with enough of the vinaigrette to coat. Taste and adjust the seasonings. Divide among salad plates:

4 cups bite-sized pieces arugula and romaine lettuce, washed and dried

Spoon the vegetables on top. Drizzle more dressing over the salads and garnish with:

Fresh basil leaves (optional)

Serve immediately.

Tart Greens with Apples, Pecans, and Buttermilk Honey Dressing

4 to 6 servings

Whisk together in a small bowl:

¼ cup cider vinegar

¼ cup sour cream

¼ cup buttermilk

3 tablespoons honey

1 teaspoon minced garlic

1 scallion, minced

Pinch of ground red pepper

Salt and ground black pepper to taste

Add in a slow, steady stream, whisking constantly:

½ cup olive oil

Combine in a salad bowl:

4 cups bite-sized pieces arugula, washed and dried

1 small head radicchio, washed, dried, and torn into bite-sized pieces

2 Belgian endives, washed, dried, and sliced lengthwise into long strips

Stir the dressing well, add just enough to moisten the greens, and toss to coat. Divide the greens among salad plates and top with:

2 Granny Smith or other tart apples, cored and very thinly sliced

½ cup pecan halves, toasted

Serve immediately.

Tomato and Mozzarella Salad (Insalata Caprese)

4 to 6 servings

Named for the island of Capri, where it was perhaps first made, this gloriously simple salad is popular all over Italy and is increasingly so in the United States. Be sure to use the ripest tomatoes, the freshest mozzarella, and the best extra-virgin olive oil you can find.

Arrange, alternating the tomato and cheese slices, on a platter:

4 large ripe tomatoes, cut into ½-inch-thick slices

12 ounces mozzarella cheese, cut into ¼-inch-thick slices

Sprinkle with:

1½ cups fresh basil leaves

Drizzle over the salad:

½ cup olive oil, preferably extra virgin

Salt to taste

Serve at once or let stand at room temperature for up to 1 hour before serving. In either case, do not refrigerate the salad.

Baked Goat Cheese and Baby Greens

4 servings

Mesclun includes many different salad greens and herbs, each varying in flavor, texture, and color. A mix might contain red- and green-tipped oakleaf lettuce, arugula, romaine lettuce, chervil, colorful red radicchio, curly white as well as green endive, escarole, and bitter dandelion greens. Add fresh herbs to this mixture (sage, dill, and tarragon are our favorites), top with baked goat cheese, serve with some toasted bread, and you have a delicious lunch or supper dish.

Preheat the oven to 400°F. Grease a small baking dish.

Refrigerate in a salad bowl:

6 cups mixed baby greens or mesclun, washed and dried

Stir together in a shallow bowl:

1 cup fine dry unseasoned breadcrumbs

1 teaspoon dried thyme

Pour into another shallow bowl:

¼ cup extra-virgin olive oil

Coat first with the olive oil and then with the breadcrumbs:

4 rounds fresh goat cheese, each about 2½ inches in diameter and ½ inch thick

Place the cheese in the baking dish and bake until golden brown and lightly bubbling, about 6 minutes. Meanwhile, prepare:

Basic Vinaigrette, 27

Toss the greens with just enough vinaigrette to coat and divide among 4 salad plates. Place a round of baked cheese in the center of each salad and serve at once.

Grilled Ratatouille Salad

6 servings

Prepare a medium-hot charcoal fire. Combine in a bowl:

2 to 4 tablespoons olive oil

2 to 3 tablespoons red wine vinegar, to taste

When the coals are covered with gray ash, coat with the oil mixture:

Twelve ½-inch-thick eggplant slices

2 fennel bulbs, quartered lengthwise

2 medium zucchini, cut lengthwise into thick slices

4 plum tomatoes

3 slender leeks (white part only), split up to the root ends and washed thoroughly

3 red, orange, or yellow bell peppers, or a combination

½ head garlic, unpeeled

Grill the vegetables, turning as needed, until the tomatoes and peppers are charred on the outside and the other vegetables are tender, about 5 minutes for the zucchini, up to 20 minutes for the garlic. Remove from the grill and let cool slightly. Peel, seed, and dice the tomatoes and bell peppers. Dice the fennel and zucchini into ½-inch pieces. Trim the root ends from the leeks and slice. Squeeze the garlic cloves from their skins and mash. Combine the vegetables, except the eggplant slices, in a bowl. Just before serving, stir in:

3 tablespoons minced fresh basil

1 tablespoon extra-virgin olive oil

Pinch of grated orange zest

Salt and ground black pepper to taste

Arrange the eggplant slices on a platter, top with the ratatouille, and serve at room temperature.

Avocado and Mango Salad

4 servings

This salad is luscious with either mango or papaya—choose whichever you find is the ripest. The mango and the avocado are the centerpieces here, not the greens.

Halve:

1 lemon

Halve, peel, and thinly slice lengthwise:

2 ripe Haas avocados

Gently rub the slices with the lemon halves. Slice vertically into segments:

1 ripe mango or papaya, peeled

Combine in a small bowl:

1 large red onion, thinly sliced

¼ cup fresh lemon juice

Pinch of salt

Whisk together in a small bowl:

½ cup olive oil

2 tablespoons fresh lemon juice

Salt and ground black pepper to taste

Toss with half of the dressing:

2 cups arugula leaves, washed and dried

Divide among chilled salad plates. Around the arugula, alternate slices of avocado and mango. Spoon the remaining dressing over the slices. Arrange the onion over the arugula. Serve immediately.

Cold Asparagus Salad with Sesame Seeds

4 to 6 servings

Asparagus spears poke through the earth in spring. If not picked, these young shoots grow into tall ferny branches with bright red berries. The thinner the shoot, the younger and, usually, the tenderer. They can be green, purple, or green and purple; cream-colored shoots have been raised deprived of sunlight. Select crisp, tightly closed stalks whose cut ends are not dry.

Whisk together in a small bowl:

3 tablespoons toasted sesame oil
4 teaspoons white wine vinegar
4 teaspoons light or dark soy sauce
2½ tablespoons sugar

Toast in a small skillet until golden brown:

4 teaspoons sesame seeds

Immediately stir into the dressing.
Place in a large pot of boiling water:

1½ pounds asparagus, peeled and cut diagonally into 2-inch pieces

Cook for no more than 1½ minutes for thin asparagus or 2½ minutes for thicker. Immediately drain and refill the pot with cold running water until all the heat has left the asparagus. Drain again and dry thoroughly. Cover and refrigerate until the salad is cold, about 1 hour. Toss with the dressing. Serve.

PEA SALAD

Prepare the dressing for *Cold Asparagus Salad with Sesame Seeds, left.* Cook 1 cup sugar snap peas in a large saucepan of boiling salted water for 2 minutes. Add ½ cup snow peas and ½ cup fresh or thawed frozen tiny green peas and cook for 1 minute. Drain, rinse, and drain again as for the asparagus. Pat dry. Toss the peas and dressing together in a bowl along with 6 cups pea shoots, washed and dried. Serve immediately.

Pita Salad (Fattoush)

4 servings

Toss together in a colander:

1 small cucumber, peeled, seeded, and cut into ½-inch cubes

1 teaspoon salt

Let stand to drain for 30 minutes. Preheat the oven to 350°F. On a baking sheet, bake until crisp and lightly browned, about 10 minutes:

Two 7-inch pita breads, split open

Break into bite-sized pieces. Press the excess water out of the cucumbers, rinse quickly, and blot dry. Combine the cucumbers in a medium bowl with:

3 medium, ripe tomatoes, chopped

1 small green bell pepper, diced

6 scallions, white and tender green parts, finely chopped

⅓ cup chopped fresh parsley

2 tablespoons chopped fresh cilantro

1 tablespoon finely chopped fresh mint

Whisk together in a small bowl:

⅓ cup olive oil, preferably extra virgin

Juice of 1 large lemon (about ¼ cup)

1 clove garlic, crushed

¼ teaspoon salt

Pour the dressing over the vegetables and toss well. Add the pita toasts, toss again, and serve immediately.

Cucumber and Yogurt Salad (Tzatziki)

4 to 6 servings

Set a very fine mesh sieve or a colander lined with several layers of cheesecloth over a bowl. Add and let drain at room temperature for at least 2 hours or, covered, in the refrigerator for up to 24 hours:

2 cups yogurt

Toss together in a colander:

1 large cucumber, peeled, seeded, and diced

1 teaspoon salt

Let stand to drain for 30 minutes. Press the excess water out of the cucumbers, rinse quickly, and blot dry. Mash together until a paste is formed:

2 cloves garlic, peeled

2 to 3 pinches of salt

Combine the yogurt, cucumbers, and garlic in a medium bowl along with:

2 to 3 teaspoons white wine vinegar

2 teaspoons chopped fresh mint

2 teaspoons snipped fresh dill

Salt and ground white pepper to taste

Drizzle over the salad:

1 tablespoon olive oil, preferably extra virgin

Jícama Salad

8 servings

The lime and ground chili peppers are the perfect complements to jícama's slightly sweet flavor.

Peel and halve lengthwise:

1 medium jícama (about 1 pound)

Lay each half on its cut side, slice ¼ inch thick, and cut the slices diagonally in half. Cut diagonally into ¼-inch-thick slices:

2 small cucumbers, halved lengthwise and seeded

Cut a slice off the stem and blossom ends of:

3 medium navel oranges

Stand the oranges on a cutting board and cut away the peel and all the white pith. Halve lengthwise, then cut crosswise into ¼-inch-thick slices. In a large bowl, toss the jícama, cucumbers, and oranges along with:

6 radishes, thinly sliced

1 small red onion, thinly sliced

Juice of 2 limes (about ⅓ cup)

Let stand for 20 minutes, then season with:

Salt to taste

To serve, spoon the salad onto a platter and drizzle the accumulated juices on top. Sprinkle with:

About 2 teaspoons ground chili pepper, preferably ancho or guajillo

About ⅓ cup coarsely chopped fresh cilantro

Sicilian Salad

4 to 6 servings

This is an easy salad to make and is just as good when made without the fennel or olives.

Cut a slice off the stem and blossom ends of:

4 medium navel oranges

Stand the oranges on a cutting board and cut away the peel and all the white pith. On a plate cut crosswise into ¼-inch-thick slices. Arrange the slices on a platter and pour the juice over them. Arrange with the orange slices:

1 small red onion, thinly sliced

3 small fennel bulbs, thinly sliced (optional)

½ cup pitted black Gaeta olives (optional)

Sprinkle with:

6 fresh mint leaves, finely chopped

Ground black pepper to taste

Drizzle over the salad:

2 tablespoons olive oil, or more to taste

Let stand for about 2 hours at room temperature before serving.

Peruvian Potato Salad

4 servings; about 1 ⅓ cups sauce

This salad is most flavorful when the potatoes are warm, but it is equally enjoyable when chilled. Use Peruvian blue potatoes if available, but any all-purpose or boiling potato will work.

Heat in a small skillet over medium heat:

1 tablespoon peanut oil

Add:

½ medium onion, chopped
1 clove garlic, chopped

Cook until soft and lightly browned, 5 to 7 minutes. Transfer to a blender and add:

½ cup roasted unsalted Spanish peanuts, skins removed

½ cup milk
⅓ cup crumbled ricotta salata or farmer's cheese
1½ tablespoons peanut oil
1 fresh jalapeño or other chili pepper, quartered and seeded
½ teaspoon salt
¼ teaspoon ground turmeric

Blend the sauce until smooth and set aside. Cover with cold water and bring to a boil:

4 to 6 Peruvian blue, Yellow Finn, or boiling potatoes (about 1½ pounds)

Cook until tender when pierced with the tip of a sharp knife, about

25 minutes. Drain and, when cool enough to handle, peel and slice into rounds.

Arrange on 4 salad plates:

Lettuce leaves

Top the lettuce with the potato slices and, if desired, season with:

Salt and ground black pepper

Spoon the reserved sauce over the potatoes. Garnish each plate with:

Hard-boiled eggs
Pickled onions
Black olives
Cooked corn on the cob, sliced into 2-inch-thick rounds

French Potato Salad

6 to 8 servings

Bring to a boil in a large pot with enough salted cold water to cover:

2 pounds red or other waxy potatoes

Reduce the heat and simmer, uncovered, until the potatoes are tender when pierced with a fork, 20 to 25 minutes. Drain, peel if desired, and cut into bite-sized pieces. Place in a medium bowl while still warm. Whisk together in a small bowl:

6 tablespoons red or white wine vinegar, or ¼ cup white wine vinegar and 2 tablespoons dry white wine

1 shallot, minced, or ½ red onion, minced, or 3 tablespoons finely snipped fresh chives

2 tablespoons minced fresh parsley

2 tablespoons drained capers (optional)

1 tablespoon whole-grain mustard

1 tablespoon minced fresh tarragon, mint, dill, or thyme (optional)

Salt and ground black pepper to taste

Add in a slow, steady stream, whisking constantly:

6 tablespoons olive oil

Pour the dressing over the potatoes, toss gently to combine, and serve warm, at room temperature, or chilled.

Tabbouleh

4 to 6 servings

Tabbouleh is a popular Middle Eastern salad.

Combine in a large bowl:

1 cup medium bulgur

2 cups boiling water

Cover with an inverted plate and let stand for 30 minutes. Drain in a sieve, pressing with the back of a large spoon to remove the excess moisture, and return to the bowl. Add:

4 large ripe tomatoes, finely chopped

2 cups fresh parsley sprigs, finely chopped

1 cup packed fresh mint sprigs, finely chopped

1 cup packed purslane, washed, dried, and finely chopped (optional)

1 bunch scallions, finely chopped

1 medium onion, finely chopped

Stir in:

½ teaspoon ground allspice (optional)

½ teaspoon salt

¼ teaspoon ground black pepper

Whisk together:

⅓ cup fresh lemon juice

⅓ cup olive oil

Add to the bulgur and toss to coat. Spoon the salad onto a platter and surround with:

1 head romaine lettuce, separated into leaves, washed, and dried

Serve at room temperature.

Couscous Salad with Pine Nuts and Raisins

4 servings

Fine bulgur, like couscous, can also be steamed and used in this recipe.

Place in a medium bowl:

1¼ cups quick-cooking couscous

Pour in:

1½ cups boiling water or stock

Cover with an inverted plate and let stand for 10 minutes. Uncover and fluff with chopsticks or a fork. Transfer to a bowl and toss with:

¼ cup *Lime Vinaigrette*, 27, prepared with cumin seeds

Add and toss to combine:

¼ cup pine nuts, toasted

1 yellow bell pepper, finely diced

6 dried apricots, finely chopped

3 tablespoons golden raisins

2 tablespoons dried currants

2 tablespoons chopped fresh cilantro or snipped fresh chives

QUINOA SALAD

Quinoa's taste and texture tease with lightness and a very faint herbal quality.
Prepare *Couscous Salad with Pine Nuts and Raisins, left,* substituting 3 cups cooked quinoa (about 1 cup uncooked) for the couscous.

Brown Rice and Tofu Salad with Orange Sesame Dressing

6 servings

Shake together in a tightly covered jar:

½ cup canola oil

4 teaspoons toasted sesame oil

⅓ cup orange juice

⅓ cup seasoned rice vinegar

1 small fresh jalapeño pepper, seeded and minced

1 teaspoon minced peeled fresh ginger

1 teaspoon minced garlic

Chill. Combine in a large bowl:

4 cups warm cooked brown basmati rice

One 10½-ounce package extra-firm tofu, pressed if desired, 80, and cut into ¾-inch cubes

3 cups cooked adzuki beans (about 1 cup dried), rinsed and drained if canned

½ cup chopped red onions

1 cup chopped bell peppers, preferably half red and half green

¼ cup finely chopped fresh cilantro

Shake the dressing well, pour over the rice mixture, and toss well to coat. Season with:

Salt and ground black pepper to taste

Line a serving platter with:

Lettuce leaves

Spoon the salad on the leaves and sprinkle with:

1 tablespoon sesame seeds, toasted

Garlic-Sesame Triticale Salad

4 servings

A hybrid of wheat and rye, triticale berries are a little larger than wheat berries and lighter in taste.

Cook in a large pot of boiling salted water until tender, about 1 hour:

1 cup triticale berries

Drain and remove to a large bowl. Heat in a small skillet over medium heat until hot but not smoking:

3 tablespoons vegetable oil

Add and cook, stirring, until very fragrant, 2 to 3 minutes:

2 scallions, minced

1 tablespoon minced peeled fresh ginger

1 or 2 cloves garlic, minced

Stir in:

½ teaspoon toasted sesame oil

Salt to taste

Red pepper flakes to taste

Stir into the triticale berries. Taste and adjust the seasonings. Serve warm or at room temperature, garnished with:

½ cup coarsely chopped dry-roasted cashews or peanuts

MAKING BEAN, RICE, AND GRAIN SALADS

The mild flavors and chewy textures of beans, rice, and other grains are a perfect backdrop for a variety of salads. Fresh vegetables and seasonings are added for contrast and flavor, making these versatile side dishes or healthy meals unto themselves. These salads take a bit of advance preparation, since the beans, rice, and grains must first be cooked, but once made, they hold up well. If the salad has been refrigerated, let it stand at room temperature for a bit before serving, taste and adjust the seasonings (starches tend to absorb seasonings over time), and serve at room temperature. Salads are best made from beans, rice, and grains that are cooked to firm-tender. Be sure everything is well drained, lest it dilute the dressing.

Rye Berry Salad with Roasted Pepper Dressing

4 to 6 servings

Rye is a good source of thiamine, iron, phosphorus, and potassium and has been considered a weight-loss aid because it retains water, swells more than other grains in the stomach, and digests more slowly, prolonging the feeling of fullness.

Place in a pot:

1½ cups water
¼ teaspoon salt
½ cup rye berries

Bring to a boil. Reduce the heat to low and simmer, covered, until some berries have burst and all are tender, 45 to 60 minutes.

Meanwhile, mash together to form a paste:

1 clove garlic, peeled
¼ teaspoon salt

Remove to a blender or food processor and add:

One 7½-ounce jar roasted red peppers, drained
6 tablespoons olive oil
2 tablespoons fresh lemon juice, or to taste
2 tablespoons white wine vinegar
1 shallot, chopped
1 tablespoon ground cumin
Salt and ground black pepper to taste
Pinch of ground red pepper

Puree until smooth. Drain the rye berries in a colander, transfer to a large bowl, and add just enough dressing to moisten. Stir to coat. Stir in:

1 large carrot, peeled and diced
2 small celery stalks with leaves, diced
6 to 8 radishes, diced
1 medium zucchini, diced
½ fennel bulb, diced
1 small yellow bell pepper, diced
½ small red onion, finely diced
2 tablespoons minced fresh cilantro
Salt and ground black pepper to taste

Add enough additional dressing to coat. Taste and adjust the seasonings. Serve at room temperature.

Chickpea Salad

4 servings

Chickpeas are rich in vitamins A and C, high in fiber, and a good source of calcium and iron.

Combine in a medium bowl:

2 cups canned chickpeas, rinsed and drained
½ small red onion, minced
3 tablespoons minced fresh parsley
2½ tablespoons fresh lemon juice
2 tablespoons extra-virgin olive oil
1 teaspoon Dijon mustard
1 to 2 cloves garlic, minced
Salt and ground black pepper to taste

On a platter, make a bed of:

4 cups shredded chicory, escarole, or romaine lettuce, washed and dried

Spoon the chickpea salad on top and serve at room temperature.

CHICKPEA AND ROASTED RED PEPPER SALAD

Prepare Chickpea Salad, left, adding 2 red bell peppers, roasted, 58, peeled, and diced, or one 7-ounce jar roasted red peppers, drained and diced, along with the onions.

Lentil and Red Potato Salad with Warm Sherry Vinaigrette

4 servings

Make this close to serving time so that it can be consumed while still warm. It goes well with braised escarole or other greens.

Cook in boiling water until tender, about 15 minutes:

12 ounces small red potatoes, halved if larger than 1 inch in diameter

Drain and cut into small cubes when cool enough to handle. Combine in a large bowl:

½ cup thinly sliced scallions
½ cup chopped fresh parsley

Add the potato cubes along with:

4½ cups warm cooked green or brown lentils (about 1½ cups dried)

Whisk together in a small saucepan:

¼ cup extra-virgin olive oil
3 tablespoons sherry vinegar
1 clove garlic, very finely minced
½ teaspoon salt
⅛ teaspoon ground black pepper

Heat, stirring, until warm. Pour over the lentil mixture and serve.

White Bean Salad with Green Olives

4 to 6 servings

Serve this salad on a bed of crisp lettuce leaves, with wedges of ripe tomato and crunchy bread sticks alongside.

Combine in a medium bowl:

3 cups cooked white kidney beans (about 1 cup dried), or other white beans, rinsed and drained if canned
2 small celery stalks, thinly sliced

15 Spanish olives, pitted and sliced
2 tablespoons chopped fresh tarragon or parsley

Whisk together:

1 tablespoon red wine vinegar
1 clove garlic, minced
½ teaspoon sweet paprika
¼ teaspoon salt

Whisk in:

3 to 4 tablespoons olive oil, preferably extra virgin

Pour the dressing over the bean mixture and toss gently to coat. Season with:

Ground black pepper to taste

Serve at room temperature.

Black Bean, Corn, and Tomato Salad

6 servings

Boil in water to cover for 1 minute:

1½ cups corn kernels (cut from 3 ears corn)

Drain and rinse under cold water. Whisk together in a small bowl:

2 tablespoons red wine vinegar
1 clove garlic, minced
⅛ teaspoon salt
Ground black pepper to taste

Gradually whisk in:

5 tablespoons olive oil, or to taste
¼ cup snipped or sliced fresh basil

Toss with most of the dressing in a serving bowl:

3 cups cooked black beans (about 1 cup dried), rinsed and drained if canned

With the remaining dressing, toss the corn along with:

8 ounces cherry tomatoes, halved
1 cup chopped red onions

Stir gently into the beans. Serve garnished with:

Fresh basil leaves

ABOUT **SANDWICHES,** WRAPS & PIZZAS

John Montagu, an eighteenth-century English diplomat and the fourth Earl of Sandwich, was an inveterate card player who disliked being taken away from his game for anything so mundane as lunch. When hunger panged, he would ask his servants for a piece of meat on top of (and perhaps also beneath) a slice of bread so he could eat without laying down his hand. Thus the sandwich got its name, and unlike so many other tales of culinary origins, this one is apparently quite true.

Even though Montagu may have been responsible for naming the sandwich, he certainly did not invent it. Almost every culture has its "sandwich," whether the burritos of Mexico, the filled pita pockets of the Middle East, or the calzones (and, by extension, pizzas—open-faced sandwiches) of Italy. Pizzas, in fact, have become America's great one-dish meal.

Grilled Eggplant and Roasted Red Pepper Panini, 42

Grilled Eggplant and Roasted Red Pepper Panini

4 sandwiches

Panini *literally means "little breads," but it is a common Italian word for sandwiches.*

Prepare a medium-hot charcoal fire or preheat the broiler.

Combine well:

6 fresh basil leaves, chopped
2 tablespoons balsamic vinegar
1 to 3 cloves garlic, minced
2 red bell peppers, roasted, 58, peeled, seeded, and cut into strips about ¼ inch thick

Cut crosswise into ½-inch-thick slices:

1 medium eggplant

Brush the eggplant slices on both sides with:

2 tablespoons olive oil

Grill the eggplant over the hot coals or broil 4 inches from the heat just until tender, about 4 minutes each side. Remove from the heat.

Split in half horizontally:

Four 4-inch squares *Focaccia, below*

Spread the bottom halves generously with:

Tapenade, below

Arrange on top:

4 ounces sliced fresh mozzarella or crumbled feta or goat cheese
1 large ripe tomato, sliced

Divide the eggplant and the pepper mixture on top and cover with the top halves of the focaccia. Press together gently and serve.

Focaccia

Two 10-inch focaccia

Like pizza, focaccia is essentially a large disk or slab of slightly risen bread dough—but focaccia is more bread and less topping. A simple way to make focaccia is to use pizza dough. Divide in half and roll each piece out to a ½-inch-thick round:

Basic pizza dough, 46

Transfer these to well-oiled 10-inch cake pans. Let rise, covered with plastic wrap, for 1½ hours.

Preheat the oven to 400°F.

Ten minutes before baking, dimple the dough with your fingertips and drizzle evenly with:

Olive oil (as much as ½ cup— authentic focaccia is quite oily)

Top with:

Dried herbs or coarse sea salt

Bake the focaccia until golden, about 25 minutes. Remove from the pans to cool on a rack and serve warm or at room temperature.

Tapenade (Caper Olive Paste)

About 2¾ cups

Based on its name, the one essential ingredient in this popular spread is the caper—tapeno in Provençal. Tapenade made without capers or with only a hint of them is sometimes called olivade.

Combine in a food processor:

2 cups black olives, preferably oil cured, pitted
3 tablespoons drained capers

3 tablespoons extra-virgin olive oil
2 tablespoons brandy or fresh lemon juice
2 cloves garlic, coarsely chopped
2 teaspoons fresh thyme leaves, or 1 teaspoon dried
Salt and ground black pepper to taste

Pulse until the mixture is still coarse but of a uniform consistency.

Grilled Vegetable Roll-Ups

4 sandwiches

Grill:

2 red bell peppers, halved

2 green bell peppers, halved

1 small eggplant, cut lengthwise into ½-inch-thick slices

2 medium red onions, cut into thick slices

1 zucchini or summer squash, cut lengthwise into ½-inch-thick slices

8 mushrooms, wiped clean

Let stand until cool enough to handle. Chop all the grilled vegetables into ¼-inch pieces and combine in a bowl with:

2 tablespoons coarsely chopped fresh basil, parsley, or cilantro

Salt and ground black pepper to taste

About ¼ cup Mojo, right, or a vinaigrette of your choice, 27

Divide among:

4 flatbreads, such as pita bread

On 2 opposite sides of the flatbread, fold over ½ inch, then roll up tightly, starting at one of the unfolded sides and serve.

Classic Bean Burritos

4 servings

These Mexican-American "roll-ups" differ from tacos primarily because flour rather than corn tortillas are used.
Preheat the oven to 350°F.
Divide into 2 batches and wrap in aluminum foil:

8 flour tortillas

Warm in the oven for 15 to 20 minutes. Remove from the oven and lay the tortillas flat on a work surface. Spoon down the middle of each, dividing evenly and leaving a margin of about 1½ inches at the bottom edge:

4 cups Refried Beans, 81

Sprinkle with:

2 cups grated Monterey Jack cheese

½ cup grated Cheddar cheese

½ cup minced onions

Minced jalapeño or other fresh chili peppers to taste

Fold the bottom of the tortilla up, then roll it from one side into a cylinder. Place the burritos on a baking sheet and bake until the cheese is melted, about 5 minutes. Serve at once. If desired, garnish with:

Sour cream

Minced scallions or snipped fresh chives

GRILLED VEGETABLE BURRITOS

Prepare *Classic Bean Burritos, above,* reducing the refried beans to 1 cup and omitting the cheeses, onions, and peppers. Top the beans on each tortilla with about ½ cup coarsely chopped mixed grilled red bell peppers, zucchini, and scallions. There is no need to heat this one—just top with 1 to 2 tablespoons fresh salsa, roll up, and serve.

Mojo

About 1 cup

The national table sauce of Cuba, mojo is a colorful version of a basic vinaigrette. Traditionally made with the fresh juice of the sour orange, it can also be made with fresh lime juice and, for variation, grapefruit or pineapple juice. Unlike most vinaigrettes, mojo is briefly cooked to bring out the full flavor of the garlic. Choose plump, firm heads of cloves with tight, papery skins. Avoid cloves with brown spots or green sprouts. To mince garlic, slice a peeled clove lengthwise, cut through once or twice horizontally, then chop crosswise into very fine pieces.

Use caution when adding the juice to the hot oil, as it may splatter. A deep saucepan is a wise precaution. Mojo can be stored for a few days, but is best when fresh.
Heat in a saucepan over medium heat:

½ cup olive oil

Add and cook until fragrant but not browned, 20 to 30 seconds:

8 cloves garlic, minced

Remove from the heat and let cool 5 minutes. Carefully stir in and bring to a boil:

¾ cup fresh lime, grapefruit, or pineapple juice

¾ teaspoon ground cumin

Salt and ground black pepper to taste

Let cool and serve at room temperature. This sauce will keep, covered and refrigerated, for up to 3 days.

Falafel

4 servings

Falafel—the original "veggie burger"—is popular street food in the Middle East and New York City. The beans are soaked, ground, and fried rather than boiled.

Pick over, rinse, and soak, 78:

1 ¼ cups dried chickpeas

Drain thoroughly. Place in a food processor and finely chop. Add:

½ cup chopped onions

¼ cup packed fresh parsley leaves

2 cloves garlic, chopped

2 teaspoons ground cumin

1 ½ teaspoons salt

½ teaspoon coriander seeds, crushed, or ½ teaspoon ground coriander

½ teaspoon baking soda

¼ teaspoon ground red pepper

Process until the mixture is coarsely pureed. Remove to a bowl and stir in:

2 tablespoons all-purpose flour

With wet hands, form the chickpea mixture into 4 patties, each about 3 inches in diameter. Let stand for 15 minutes.

Meanwhile, preheat the oven to 350°F.

Pour into a deep skillet:

½ inch vegetable oil

Fry the chickpea patties until golden on both sides, about 4 minutes each side. Drain on paper towels. Stir together:

¼ cup tahini

¼ cup cold water

1 tablespoon fresh lemon juice

Pinch of salt

Wrap in aluminum foil:

4 pita breads

Heat in the oven until warmed, about 10 minutes. Open one edge of each pita bread and distribute among the pockets:

2 cups thinly sliced crisp lettuce (such as romaine or iceberg), washed and dried

4 thin tomato slices

Add a falafel to each pita and drizzle the tahini sauce over the falafel. Add:

Hot red pepper sauce to taste

Hummus (Middle Eastern Chickpea and Sesame Dip)

About 2 cups

If using canned chickpeas, rinse 2 cups (one 16-ounce can) and puree as directed, using water to thin the puree. In Egypt, hummus is flavored with cumin; use ½ teaspoon ground cumin for this quantity.

Pick over, rinse, and soak, 78:

¾ cup dried chickpeas

Drain and place in a pan with water to cover by 2 inches. Bring to a boil, reduce the heat, and simmer until very tender, about 1½ hours. Drain, reserving the cooking liquid. Remove the chickpeas to a food processor or blender and add:

⅓ cup fresh lemon juice

3 tablespoons tahini

2 cloves garlic, finely minced

Salt to taste

Puree until smooth, adding 2 to 3 tablespoons of the cooking liquid as needed to obtain a soft, creamy consistency. Remove to a shallow serving bowl and garnish with:

1 tablespoon olive oil

1 tablespoon finely chopped fresh parsley

Sprinkling of hot or sweet paprika

Serve with:

Warm pita bread

Baba Ghanoush (Roasted Eggplant Dip)

About 2 cups

You can stir ½ cup yogurt into the eggplant puree just before serving, then garnish.

Preheat the oven to 400°F.

Pierce in several places:

3 medium eggplants (about 4 pounds)

Roast on a baking sheet until the skins are dark mahogany in color and the flesh feels soft, 45 to 60 minutes. Let stand until cool enough to handle. Split the eggplants and scoop the flesh into a colander. Press lightly to extract the excess liquid. Remove to a food processor and add:

1½ tablespoons tahini

2 cloves garlic, chopped

Juice of 1 large lemon

½ teaspoon salt

Pulse until smooth. Taste and adjust the seasonings. Remove to a shallow serving bowl and garnish with:

1 tablespoon olive oil

1 tablespoon finely chopped fresh parsley

Several pitted black olives (optional)

Serve with:

Warm pita bread

Whipped Feta with Roasted Peppers

About 2 cups

Combine in a food processor:

1 pound Greek feta cheese, crumbled

2 tablespoons extra-virgin olive oil

Pulse until the feta is creamy. Add:

1 red bell pepper, roasted, 58, peeled, seeded, and coarsely chopped

2 or 3 fresh jalapeño peppers, seeded and minced

2 pickled pepperoncini, rinsed, seeded, and minced

Several grindings of black pepper

Pulse until the mixture is well combined while gradually adding:

3 tablespoons extra-virgin olive oil

2 tablespoons fresh lemon juice

The feta should be creamy and spreadable. Taste and add more olive oil and/or lemon juice if desired. Serve with:

Crackers or pita bread

PEPPERONCINI

These sweet to mildly piquant pale green to red peppers are best known as a pickled pepper used in Italian dishes. They rarely are found fresh in markets but are popular with many home gardeners. They measure about 3 inches in length and ¾ inch wide at the stem end, sloping gently to a point.

Pizza with Tomato Sauce and Mozzarella

Two 12-inch pizzas

This pizza has a relatively thick crust. We advise not overloading your pizza with sauce and cheese.

Combine in a large mixing bowl or the bowl of a heavy-duty mixer and let stand until the yeast is dissolved, about 5 minutes:

1 package (2¼ teaspoons) active dry yeast

1⅓ cups warm (105° to 115°F) water

Add:

3½ to 3¾ cups all-purpose flour

2 tablespoons olive oil

1 tablespoon salt

1 tablespoon sugar (optional)

Mix by hand or on low speed for about 1 minute to blend all the ingredients. Knead for about 10 minutes by hand or with the dough hook on low to medium speed until the dough is smooth and elastic. Transfer the dough to a bowl lightly coated with olive oil and turn it over once to coat with oil. Cover with plastic wrap and let rise in a warm place (75° to 80°F) until doubled in volume, 1 to 1½ hours. Preheat the oven to 475°F. Grease and dust 2 baking sheets with cornmeal; or place a baking stone (if you have one) in the oven and preheat it for 45 minutes. Punch the dough down and divide it in half. Roll each piece into a ball and let rest, loosely covered with plastic wrap, for 10 to 15 minutes.

Flatten each ball of dough 1 at a time on a lightly floured work surface into a 12-inch round, rolling and stretching the dough. Place each dough circle on a prepared baking sheet; if using a baking stone, place them on baker's peels dusted with cornmeal. Lift the edge and pinch it to form a lip. To prevent the filling from making the crust soggy, brush the top of the dough with:

Olive oil

Use your fingertips to push dents in the surface of the dough (to prevent bubbling) and let rest for about 10 minutes. Spread in an even layer on each pizza, leaving a ½-inch border:

½ cup Italian Tomato Sauce, right

Sprinkle each with:

6 ounces mozzarella cheese, shredded

If using a baking stone, slide the pizza off the baker's peel onto the baking stone in the preheated oven. If making the pizza on a baking sheet, place the pan and pizza in the oven on the bottom rack. Bake until the crust is browned and the cheese is golden, about 12 minutes. Remove from the oven, slice, and serve at once.

PIZZA WITH FENNEL, ONION, AND ASIAGO CHEESE

Prepare dough as above, and spread with Italian Tomato Sauce, right, *before adding this topping.*
Sauté 1 medium onion, sliced; 1 fennel bulb, trimmed and sliced; and 2 cloves garlic, minced, in 2 tablespoons olive oil along with ½ teaspoon dried marjoram and ¼ teaspoon red pepper flakes until the onions are translucent, 5 to 7 minutes. Spread evenly over the pizzas. Season to taste with salt and ground black pepper and bake as directed. Five minutes before the pizza is done, sprinkle ½ cup grated Asiago cheese over the top.

Italian Tomato Sauce

This classic tomato sauce can be kept in the refrigerator for up to 4 days or frozen for up to 3 months. It puts ripe garden tomatoes to excellent use.

Heat in a large skillet over medium heat:

2 to 3 tablespoons extra-virgin olive oil

Add:

⅓ cup finely chopped fresh parsley

1 medium onion, finely chopped

1 small carrot, peeled and finely chopped

1 celery stalk with leaves, finely chopped

Cook, stirring, until the onions are golden brown, about 5 minutes. Add:

2 cloves garlic, minced

½ cup packed fresh basil leaves, chopped, or 1 sprig each fresh rosemary, sage, and thyme

Cook, stirring, for about 30 seconds. Stir in:

2½ pounds ripe tomatoes, peeled, if desired, seeded, and coarsely chopped, or one 28-ounce can and one 14-ounce can whole tomatoes, with juice, crushed between your fingers as you add them to the pan

1 tablespoon tomato paste (optional)

Salt and ground black pepper to taste

Simmer, uncovered, until the sauce is thickened, about 10 minutes. Remove the herb sprigs.

Calzone with Portobello Mushrooms and Goat Cheese

2 calzones; 4 servings

Calzone, literally "pant leg," is a pizza folded onto itself—a closed envelope of dough with the toppings on the inside.
Prepare through the first rise:
Basic pizza dough, opposite
Preheat the oven to 450°F. Lightly grease a baking sheet.
Divide the dough in half and form each half into a ball. Place on a lightly floured work surface, sprinkle with flour, and cover with a dish towel or plastic wrap. Let stand for 20 minutes.
Meanwhile, sauté until tender:
1 tablespoon olive oil
2 large portobello mushrooms, thinly sliced
8 to 10 button mushrooms, thinly sliced
1 red onion, thinly sliced

3 cloves garlic, minced
Let cool and season with:
Salt and ground black pepper to taste
Shape each ball of dough into a thick disk and let stand for about 5 minutes. Roll each one into a 10-inch round. Divide the filling between the rounds. Sprinkle evenly with:
½ teaspoon dried thyme
4 ounces goat cheese, crumbled
Fold the dough over, making a half circle, and tightly seal the edges with your fingertips. Reduce the oven temperature to 400°F. Place the calzones on the baking sheet and bake until nicely browned, 30 to 35 minutes. Serve hot or at room temperature.

White Pizza with Potatoes and Sage

Two 12-inch pizzas

According to American labeling laws, if it does not have tomato sauce, you cannot call it pizza. This would astonish some Italians, who frequently eat their pizza with just a touch of tomato or even none at all.
Prepare as directed:
Basic pizza dough, opposite
Brush each generously with:
Extra-virgin olive oil
Top each with:
8 ounces potatoes, boiled and very thinly sliced while still warm
2 teaspoons dried or 2 tablespoons coarsely chopped fresh sage

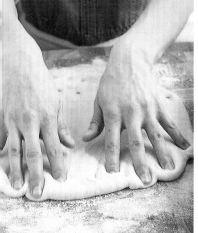

2 tablespoons extra-virgin olive oil
Salt and ground black pepper to taste
If using a baking stone, slide the pizza off the baker's peel onto the baking stone in the preheated oven. If making the pizza on a baking sheet, place the pan and pizza in the oven on the bottom rack. Bake until the crust is golden brown, about 12 minutes. Remove from the oven, slice, and serve at once.

Grilled Pizza with Tomato and Three Cheeses

One 10- to 12-inch pizza

Grilling pizza requires a hot fire started with kindling and fueled with hardwood charcoal. Build your fire on one side of the grill. For cooking, you will want a cool area on the grill in order to add the toppings without burning the bottom of the crust. For kettle-type grills, create a center line with two or three bricks laid end to end and bank the charcoal on one side. If your grill cannot accommodate a 12-inch round of dough, simply divide the dough and make 2 or 3 small pizzas. Set up your work area as close to the grill as possible. The dough, olive oil, and a variety of topping ingredients should be close at hand and ready before you begin. This recipe will serve four as an appetizer or one as a main course. The dough can easily be doubled or tripled.

Combine in a mixing bowl or in the bowl of a heavy-duty mixer:

1 teaspoon active dry yeast
2 tablespoons warm (105° to 115°F) water

Let stand until the yeast is dissolved and the water is foamy on the surface, about 5 minutes. Add:

⅔ cup cool water
2 cups unbleached all-purpose flour
1½ teaspoons coarse salt

Mix until the dough comes together. Knead by hand or with the dough hook on medium speed until the dough is smooth and elastic, about 10 minutes. Brush a large bowl with:

Olive oil

Add the dough and brush the surface with:

Olive oil

Cover the bowl with plastic wrap and let rise in a warm place away from drafts until doubled in volume,

about 2 hours. Punch the dough down. Cover with plastic wrap and let rise for at least 45 minutes at room temperature or overnight in the refrigerator.

While the dough is rising, prepare a hot charcoal fire, setting the grill rack 3 to 4 inches above the coals. Prepare the topping ingredients. Brush the back side of a large baking sheet with:

1 tablespoon olive oil

Place 1 ball of dough on the pan and turn it over to coat with oil. With your hands, spread and flatten the pizza dough into a 10- to 12-inch freeform circle, ¼ inch thick. You may end up with a rectangle rather than a circle; the shape is unimportant. If the dough shrinks back into itself, let it stand for a few minutes, then continue to spread and flatten the dough. Do not make a lip. Take care not to stretch the dough so thin that it tears. If this happens, all is not lost; rather than try to repair the holes, simply avoid them when adding the toppings. When the fire is hot (you will be able to hold your hand 5 inches above the fire for only 3 to 4 seconds), use your fingertips to lift the dough gently by the 2 corners closest to you and drape it onto the coolest part of the grill rack. Catch the loose edge on the grill first and guide the remaining dough into place over the fire. Cover, and within 2 to 3 minutes, the dough will puff slightly, the underside will stiffen, and grill marks will appear. Using spring-loaded tongs and a spatula, immediately flip the crust over onto the coolest part of the grill. Quickly

brush the grilled surface with:

2 teaspoons olive oil

Spread over the entire surface of the pizza:

¼ cup grated Parmesan cheese
⅓ cup grated fontina cheese
2 tablespoons grated pecorino cheese

Spoon in dollops on top:

6 tablespoons chopped canned tomatoes in heavy puree

Top with:

1 tablespoon chopped fresh parsley
1 teaspoon ground black pepper

Sprinkle on top:

1 to 2 tablespoons olive oil

After the toppings have been added, slide the pizza back toward the hot coals so that about half of the pizza is directly over the heat. Rotate the pizza frequently so that different sections receive high heat and check the underside by lifting the edge with tongs to be sure it is not burning. The pizza is done when the top is bubbling and the cheese is melted. Garnish with:

5 fresh basil leaves, torn by hand

Serve immediately.

MIXED HERBS AND CHEESE PIZZA

Liberally brush the grilled side of the pizza with olive oil. Top with ½ cup grated fontina cheese, 2 tablespoons grated pecorino cheese, ½ teaspoon minced fresh garlic, ¼ cup chopped mixed fresh herbs (oregano, thyme, basil, rosemary), and ¼ cup chopped fresh parsley. Drizzle 2 to 3 tablespoons olive oil over the top. Finish grilling as directed.

ABOUT
VEGETABLES

It is a glorious time for vegetable lovers. Farmers at their markets, exporters, and seedsmen are showering us with tastes, textures, and aromas we had never even heard of a few years ago. Science keeps confirming the age-old maternal admonition to eat your vegetables. The specific diseases you can avoid and the miracle micronutrient of the moment might change with each new study, but the general consensus stays the same: Vegetables are good for you. Every vegetable contains every nutrient—every vitamin (with the exception of vitamin B_{12}, which vegetarians can obtain easily from dairy products), every mineral, every kind of dietary fiber. It is less important to worry about which vegetable has the higher amount of one vitamin or antioxidant than to eat as many vegetables as you can, the fresher the better.

June Vegetable Ragout, 75

Buying and Keeping Fresh Vegetables

Avoid vegetables that look dry or wrinkled, bruised or badly blemished. If two vegetables are of equal size and one is heavier, the heavier vegetable, which retains more moisture, will be more succulent. A good rule to follow is to select vegetables as close to the same size as possible—this ensures even cooking, even when pieces are cut up.

Because vegetables are generally less fragile than fruits, they are permitted to ripen before harvest. Fresh vegetables are still very much alive when you bring them into the kitchen. A cold, moist environment helps keep their tissues vibrant. For most vegetables, the shelter of a sealed perforated plastic bag (sold as "vegetable" bags) in a closed refrigerator crisper is ideal. However, if there is too much moisture, tissues start to deteriorate. For this reason, wait until just before cooking them to wash vegetables.

Here are a few points for storing fresh vegetables. **Buds and stems:** Plunge the stalks of artichokes, asparagus, broccoli, and cauliflower and any long-stemmed greens in a pitcher of water, then refrigerate. **Greens without stems:** Whether for salad or cooking, wrap in barely moist paper towels, then place in a perforated vegetable bag. **Roots:** Cut off any greens on top, leaving 2 to 3 inches of stems. Wrap the greens separately. Leaves draw moisture from their roots—an advantage for the leaves, but not the roots. **Mushrooms:** Wrap these in a loose paper bag.

If the vegetable comes wrapped in cellophane, remove the wrapper and place the vegetable in a perforated plastic bag. The following vegetables are best stored in a cool, dry place—ideally somewhere between 45° and 50°F, but a warmer temperature is better than a colder one: boniatos, eggplants, garlic, onions, plantains, potatoes, winter squashes, sweet potatoes, taro roots, tomatoes, yams, and yuca roots.

Preparing Vegetables

Prepare vegetables as close to cooking time as possible. All vegetables grown commercially and most you grow yourself—even organically raised vegetables—should be washed before preparing. Only the insides of layered vegetables (lettuces, cabbages, onions) can be presumed to be free of dust and the errant insect. Wash vegetables no more than is needed to remove dust and dirt. Root vegetables whose peel you will retain should be scrubbed with a fairly stiff brush—you can see the soil melt away. Do not use a woven plastic or metal pad to scrub vegetables, as brittle bits of the pad can break off and get buried, unseen, in the food. In bunches of greens where soil gathers at the base, cut off the base, separate the leaves, and drop them into a sinkful of tepid, not cold, water. Tepid water relaxes the leaves just enough for them to let down hidden grains of sand. Swish gently with your hands. Individual leaves such as those of mustard greens can be rinsed individually. Lift the greens into a colander; empty the water and check for sand at the bottom of the sink; rinse the sink and repeat until the bottom is clean. With some greens, it will be necessary to repeat several times.

If you suspect the vegetable has been treated with wax and/or pesticide, the best approach is to wash it, peel it, and wash it again. Pesticide residue cannot be washed off most vegetables. Guidelines for peeling and cutting vegetables vary by vegetable type. Information on both procedures follows.

Peeling Vegetables

The skin is a vegetable's seal, keeping nutrients in and microorganisms out. Break that seal—do whatever cutting and slicing is needed—as close to cooking as possible. If necessary, vegetables can be cut up and refrigerated in an airtight container several hours in advance. Packaged precut vegetables such as carrot sticks usually have been treated with an anti-spoilage solution, and sensitive palates can taste it. Leave the skin on a vegetable whenever possible, unless you suspect it has been sprayed or waxed. The most efficient tool for peeling thin skin is a carbon-steel swivel-bladed peeler, which keeps its sharp edge over time; supermarket swivel-bladed peelers are fine but should be replaced every few months. Pare as thinly as possible. A paring knife invariably takes more flesh of the vegetable along with it than is necessary. If the vegetable is cooked whole and then peeled and sliced, maximum nutrients and flavor are retained, and the skin is easier to remove.

A few vegetables, notably potatoes, artichokes, salsify, celery root, Jerusalem artichokes, and some tropical roots, darken when their flesh is exposed to air. With these vegetables use only a stainless-steel blade—carbon steel will react with the flesh and darken it instantly. Darkened flesh is harmless, but to prevent susceptible flesh from discoloring, drop the pared vegetable into cold water mixed with lemon or lime juice or vinegar (1 tablespoon juice or vinegar to 4 cups water) for no more than 20 minutes, lest nutrients and flavor start leaching out.

HOW TO CHOP AN ONION

When chopping onions, tears can be reduced by chilling onions before peeling, or by peeling them under running water. To peel, use the tip of a sharp paring knife to pull the skin of the onion, then pull off any membrane underneath. Some cooks opt to chop onions in the food processor, but hand chopping keeps pieces drier and more uniform in shape. Cutting an onion chef's style keeps pieces from scattering all over the board and gives you control of the size of the pieces.

1 Halve the peeled onion lengthwise. Lay the halves cut side down on the board. Steady the piece lightly with the tips of the fingers of your assisting hand (the rest of your hand safely turned under, so just the first joints of the hand are exposed to the knife). Slice the onion lengthwise in parallel cuts up to, but not through, the root. (For slices, now cut off the root.)

2 Next, make several horizontal cuts of the desired thickness parallel to the board up to, but not through, the root. (For matchsticks, now cut off the root.)

3 For diced or chopped pieces, cut through the onion at right angles to the last cuts at the desired thickness, then cut through the root.

Cutting Vegetables

For uniform pieces that will finish cooking at the same time, cut by hand, with the slicing disk on a food processor, or with a mandoline. When a vegetable has two parts with distinctly different shapes and textures, as broccoli does, you must cut the denser, slower-cooking part into smaller pieces than the more tender part if both are to cook in the same amount of time. The same is true when cooking two or more vegetables together, as when steaming rutabagas and potatoes before mashing them. Chop them into pieces—the rutabagas slightly smaller, as they take a little longer to cook than potatoes—and arrange them in the steamer. Another reason for cutting vegetables is to expose just the right amount of surface to the seasoning you have in mind.

All hand cutting begins with slicing. Many chopping and slicing devices are available, but nothing can replace a skilled, relaxed wrist and a sharp, heavy knife. Practice with a mushroom, which is yielding and not slippery when placed cap down,

and work up to an onion, which can be both resistant and evasive.

The point of the knife is never lifted from the cutting board; instead it forms a pivot. The knife handle is raised high enough to be eased gently up and down, its wide blade guided by the perpendicular forefinger and midfinger of the free hand, which holds and guides the vegetable being cut. As the slicing progresses, inch a slow retreat with the free hand, which should keep a firm grasp on the object. When roll-cutting, make a diagonal cut straight down, roll the carrot (or turnip or potato) a quarter turn, and slice again. Repeat until all of the carrot is cut.

It is easier to slice a round vegetable, like a potato, if you first cut a thin slice off the bottom to create a flat surface to rest on the cutting board (the resulting slices will not be completely round, however). For attractive diagonal slices of a thin vegetable, such as green beans or asparagus, hold the knife at an angle to either the vegetable or the

cutting board. For most everyday cooking, vegetables are simply sliced crosswise; they can first be cut lengthwise into halves or quarters if they are very thick. But if you want to turn slices into more elegant strips or cubes, cut long vegetables, like zucchini, into 2-inch chunks and then slice the pieces lengthwise (for the tidiest appearance, first cut a straight edge on all sides of chunks and discard the scraps—or save them for the stockpot). Round vegetables, like turnips, can be sliced crosswise or lengthwise, depending on which will yield the longer slice.

To cut slices into smaller pieces, stack them, a few at a time, then cut them into very thin strips (less than ⅛ inch thick) to make a julienne, slightly wider strips (about ⅛ inch thick) to make matchsticks, or much wider strips (about ¼ inch thick) to make batons. To dice the vegetable, cut first into ½-inch-wide strips, then hold them together and cut across them to make ½-inch cubes or tiny ⅛-inch cubes.

Chard Sautéed with Garlic

4 to 6 servings

Remove the stems from:

2 medium bunches red or green chard (about 1½ pounds)

Cut the stems into ½-inch pieces. Coarsely chop the leaves; rinse well, but do not dry. Heat in a large skillet over medium-low heat until the oil smells good and the garlic is just beginning to color:

2 tablespoons extra-virgin olive oil
2 cloves garlic, thinly sliced
1 small dried red chili pepper, crumbled, or ¼ to ½ teaspoon red pepper flakes (optional)

Add the chard stems and season with:

Salt to taste

Cook, stirring occasionally, until the stems are nearly tender, about 2 minutes. Add the chard leaves and cook, partially covered, until both the leaves and the stems are tender, 3 to 5 minutes more. Season with:

Juice of ½ lemon or 1½ tablespoons red wine vinegar

Taste again for salt. Serve in a bowl, surrounded with:

Lemon wedges

Sautéed Broccoli with Garlic and Red Pepper Flakes

4 servings

A southern Italian way of fixing all kinds of vegetables. You can toss the cooked broccoli with pasta, pitted black olives, and grated Parmesan or pecorino cheese to make a main course.

Remove the florets, then peel and dice the stems of:

2 pounds broccoli

Steam or boil until barely tender, then drain. If not finishing the dish until later, cool the broccoli under cold running water. Heat in a large skillet:

3 tablespoons extra-virgin olive oil

Add and cook, stirring over medium heat until their aromas are released:

2 cloves garlic, thinly sliced or chopped

2 good pinches of red pepper flakes or 1 small dried red chili pepper, crumbled

Add the broccoli and cook until heated through and tender, 3 to 4 minutes longer. Season with:

Salt and ground black pepper to taste

Sautéed Tiny New Potatoes

4 servings

Watch your farmers' market for the first little new potatoes arriving around July.

Scrub well and pat dry:

24 very small new potatoes, about the same size

Heat in a large, heavy skillet:

2 tablespoons olive oil or clarified butter

Roll the potatoes around the pan to coat them, then cover and cook over low heat until tender, about 25 minutes. Every so often give the pan a gentle shake so that they brown evenly. Sprinkle with:

Salt and ground black pepper to taste

Snipped fresh chives, chopped fresh parsley, or other fresh herb (optional)

Stir-Fry of Napa Cabbage and Carrots

4 servings

Heat a wok or large skillet over high heat. Add and stir-fry for a few seconds, but do not allow the garlic to brown:

1 tablespoon peanut or vegetable oil

2 cloves garlic, minced

1 tablespoon minced peeled fresh ginger

Add and stir-fry for 3 minutes:

8 ounces carrots, shredded

Then add and stir-fry until the cabbage is tender, about 3 more minutes:

1 medium-large head Napa cabbage (about 2 pounds), rinsed and thinly sliced

Add and stir well to mix:

2 tablespoons light or dark soy sauce

1 teaspoon toasted sesame oil

½ teaspoon chili paste with garlic or ¼ teaspoon red pepper flakes (optional)

Serve immediately, sprinkled with:

Minced fresh cilantro or parsley

STIR-FRYING

Vegetables cut in small, even pieces and stirred over intensely high heat with a modicum of fat and liquid cook through in the fastest possible time. Stir-frying is most efficient when the pieces of food have plenty of room to move in the pan, allowing surfaces constant exposure to heat. Work in several batches, if necessary, to prevent vegetables from being crowded and steaming in their own moisture, which prevents browning and dilutes flavor. Many vegetables are best stir-fried until golden or brown and then finished with steam by adding liquid and covering the pan. This method reduces the amount of fat needed and yields excellent taste. For best results, the vegetables should be sliced to uniform thickness. Cut those that tend to stringiness on a diagonal. Stem ends and midribs should be removed from coarse-leaf vegetables, then sliced and cooked separately. Use 1 to 2 tablespoons cooking oil—peanut oil is a great favorite—per pound of vegetables.

Stir-Fried Bok Choy with Mushrooms

4 to 6 servings

Place in a small bowl:

6 dried shiitake mushrooms

Pour over the mushrooms:

½ cup boiling water

Let soak for 20 minutes, stirring the mushrooms occasionally. While the mushrooms soak, prepare, keeping the stems separate from the leafy parts:

1½ to 2 pounds bok choy, bottoms trimmed, stalks washed, and cut into 2-inch pieces

In a small saucepan, warm over medium-low heat:

1 cup *Vegetable Stock*, 17

½ teaspoon salt

½ teaspoon sugar

Remove the mushrooms from their soaking liquid and reserve the liquid. Cut the mushrooms into ¼-inch-thick slices and set aside. In a small bowl, mix:

2 tablespoons reserved mushroom soaking liquid, strained

1 tablespoon Scotch whisky or Shaoxing wine

2 teaspoons cornstarch

¾ teaspoon ground white pepper

Heat in a wok or a large skillet over high heat:

3 tablespoons peanut oil

Add the reserved mushrooms and bok choy stems and cook, stirring often, for 3 to 5 minutes to soften. Add the reserved bok choy leaves and warmed vegetable stock, cover, and steam until the leaves wilt, 1 to 2 minutes. Uncover and transfer the vegetables with a slotted spoon to a serving dish. Stir the reserved cornstarch mixture and whisk into the stock. Bring to a boil, whisking, and add:

2 teaspoons toasted sesame oil

Stir well, pour the sauce over the vegetables, and serve.

Stir-Fried Yard-Long Beans with Ginger and Garlic

4 servings

Yard-long beans keep their firm-crunchy texture when stir-fried. Select thin, dark green beans—as opposed to the lighter-colored beans—for best flavor.

Heat a wok over high heat for 30 seconds. Add:

2 tablespoons peanut oil

Swirl the wok to coat it with the oil and heat until the oil is hot. Add:

1 pound yard-long beans or green beans, trimmed and cut to the desired length

1 tablespoon minced peeled fresh ginger

2 teaspoons minced fresh garlic

¼ teaspoon salt, or to taste

Stir-fry until the beans are bright green, 5 to 6 minutes. Do not allow the garlic to burn. Add:

3 to 4 tablespoons rich stock or water

Cover and simmer gently until the beans are tender, 8 to 10 minutes.

Roasting Peppers

Roasting provides the best way to remove the skin of peppers. In addition, it softens their flesh, tempers the raw taste, and adds a delicious smokiness. Thick-walled peppers can be taken a step further and charred. Thinner-walled peppers—this includes most chilies—are better if blistered but not completely charred, or they will lose flesh when you peel them. Red peppers tend to char faster than green ones, having more sugars in their flesh. Once they are blistered, lay peppers in a bowl and cover with a towel, plate, or plastic wrap. Leave for a few minutes. Their heat will create steam, which will loosen the skins. Try not to rinse peppers after roasting, for much of the smoky flavor is on the surface.

Scrape off the skins with a knife. If the peppers were whole, make a slit down one side, then run the tip of a small serrated knife around the stem underneath its base. Remove the top and the core and seeds that come with it, then scrape away remaining seeds and cut away the membranes. Add any juices in the bottom of the bowl to the dish you are making, or blend them into a vinaigrette dressing. Roasting and peeling can be done a day or two in advance; wrap the peppers airtight and refrigerate.

Stove-Roasting Fresh Peppers: This is the simplest method. Place whole peppers directly in the flames of your gas burner on its highest setting. Keep an eye on the peppers and turn them frequently with tongs, letting the peppers blister or char (do not pierce with a cooking fork, as juices will be lost). Continue until the entire surface is blistered.

Many cooks quickly stove-roast dried chili peppers before rehydrating them. A flash of intense heat deepens and rounds out flavors.

Broiler-Roasting Fresh Peppers: Line a broiler pan with aluminum foil. Place whole peppers on the foil and brush with olive oil. Broil, turning as needed, until blackened on all sides.

Grill-Roasting Fresh Peppers: This is the most flavorful method for roasting peppers. Set whole peppers on a rack over ash-covered coals, a hot but dying fire. Let them sit in one place until they are blistered or charred, then turn them and repeat until the whole pepper is done.

Griddle- or Skillet-Roasting Fresh Peppers: This is for small fresh chilies such as serranos and jalapeños. Heat a dry cast-iron griddle or skillet over high heat, add the whole peppers, and shake them around the skillet until their skins are soft and charred here and there. These chilies are customarily not peeled after roasting, but can be.

Roasted Portobello Mushrooms, Fines Herbes

About 4 servings

Brief high-heat roasting draws out just enough moisture to intensify the good flavor of these fine mushrooms. Any large, thick, fleshy caps roast success-fully—thin mushrooms can turn leath-ery. Choose clean caps—water can be absorbed by the tissues, diluting the flavor.

Position a rack in the center of the oven. Preheat the oven to 500°F. Gently wipe the tops of:

Four 4-ounce portobello or
1 pound cremini mushrooms

Trim off the stems at the caps (save for another use). Brush the bottom of a rimmed baking sheet and the tops of the caps with:

About 4 tablespoons (½ stick)
unsalted butter, melted, or
olive oil

Arrange the caps rounded side up in the pan and roast for 6 minutes.

Remove from the oven, closing the oven door, and quickly turn the caps over with tongs, rearranging cremini mushrooms, if using, in the pan. Sprinkle with:

2 tablespoons melted unsalted
butter or olive oil
Salt and ground black pepper
to taste

Return to the oven and roast until the caps look evenly roasted, 5 to 6 minutes more. Serve as a first course on small hot plates, rounded side up, drizzled with pan juices (if any) and sprinkled with a portion of the following mixture:

1 tablespoon chopped fresh chives
1 tablespoon chopped fresh chervil
1 tablespoon chopped fresh parsley
1 tablespoon chopped scallions
1 tablespoon chopped fresh
tarragon

PREPARING MUSHROOMS

Clean mushrooms with a soft brush or wipe with a damp cloth. Or if the mushrooms are truly grimy, rinse them quickly under cold running water and pat dry. Never soak mushrooms—their delicate tissues will absorb water. If desired, slice ⅛ inch off the bottom of the stems to refresh them but do not discard the flavorful stems. If only caps are called for in a recipe, cut the stem flush with the cap. Either chop the stems fairly fine, toss them until lightly browned in a little butter, and add them to the dish or use within a day to flavor something else. As a general rule, use intense heat—sauté, stir-fry, grill, broil—when cooking mushrooms, and cook just enough to lightly brown them and heat them through.

Roasted Potatoes, Beets, and Onions Vinaigrette

6 servings

Preheat the oven to 375°F.
Toss together and arrange in a single layer in a baking pan:

12 fingerling or creamer potatoes,
halved or quartered lengthwise
12 cloves garlic, unpeeled
2 tablespoons olive oil
Fresh rosemary or thyme sprigs
Salt and ground black pepper
to taste

Toss together and arrange in another baking pan:

8 ounces pearl or cipolline
onions, peeled

1 tablespoon olive oil
Salt and ground black pepper
to taste

Toss together and arrange in a third baking pan:

12 ounces baby red or golden
chiogga beets, trimmed and
scrubbed
1 tablespoon olive oil
Salt and ground black pepper
to taste

Tightly cover each pan with foil and roast the vegetables until tender, 35 to 40 minutes; uncover the

potatoes and garlic after 20 minutes to allow them to brown and crisp slightly. Reserve any juices from the beets and onions and stir into:

Basic Vinaigrette, 27

While the beets are still warm, gently rub their skins off, using paper towels. Arrange the roasted vegetables around a mound of:

1 cup loosely packed mixed fresh
herbs

Drizzle the vinaigrette over the vegetables. Serve at room temperature.

Ratatouille

4 to 6 servings

This Provençal vegetable mélange can be served warm as an entrée with saffron rice.

Sauté in a large skillet or Dutch oven over high heat until the vegetables are golden and just tender, 10 to 12 minutes:

¼ cup olive oil
1 medium eggplant (about 1 pound), peeled and cut into 1-inch cubes
1 pound zucchini, cut into 1-inch cubes

Remove the vegetables and reduce the heat to medium-high. In the same pan, cook until the onions are slightly softened:

2 tablespoons olive oil
1½ cups sliced onions

Add and cook, stirring occasionally, until the vegetables are just tender but not browned, 8 to 12 minutes:

2 large red bell peppers, cut into 1-inch squares
3 cloves garlic, chopped

Season with:

Salt and ground black pepper to taste

Add:

1½ cups chopped seeded peeled fresh tomatoes
2 to 3 sprigs fresh thyme
1 bay leaf

Reduce the heat to low, cover, and cook for 5 minutes. Add the eggplant and zucchini and cook until everything is tender, about 20 minutes more. Taste and adjust the seasonings. Stir in:

¼ cup chopped fresh basil

HOW TO PEEL AND SEED TOMATOES

1 To peel tomatoes, cut a small X in the bottom of each one—do not cut the flesh.

2 Ease the tomatoes one by one into a pot of boiling water. Leave ripe tomatoes in for about 15 seconds, barely ripe tomatoes in for twice as long. Lift the tomatoes out with a sieve and drop into a bowl of ice water to stop the cooking. Pull off the skin with the tip of the knife. If the skin sticks, return the tomato to the boiling water for another 10 seconds and repeat. If the dish can use a touch of smoky flavor and if you have a gas burner, an easier way to peel tomatoes is to hold the tomato on a long-handled fork over the burner, turning it until the skin splits. Do not plunge the tomatoes in water, but after cooling, peel as above.

3 To seed and juice tomatoes, cut each one crosswise in half (between the top and bottom). Squeeze each half gently, cut side down, over a strainer set in a bowl. Now run the tip of a finger into each of the cavities and flick out the mass of seeds.

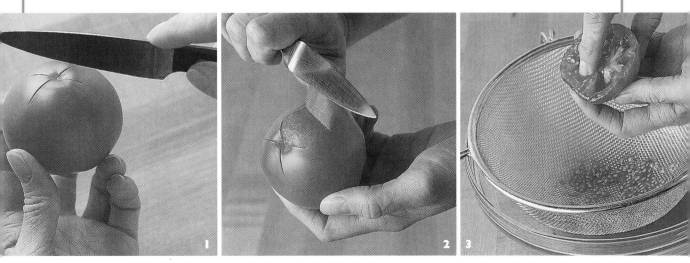

Root Vegetable Puree

4 to 6 servings

The potatoes lend this puree a light texture and delicate flavor.

Place in a large saucepan:

8 ounces all-purpose or baking potatoes, peeled and thinly sliced

Add water to cover generously, bring to a boil, and cook for 5 minutes. Add:

1 pound carrots, peeled, halved, and cut into thick slices

Continue cooking until both vegetables are completely tender, about 25 minutes. Drain and return the vegetables to the pan. Working over low heat, mash the vegetables with a potato masher or beat with a hand-held mixer until very smooth. Mix in:

½ cup milk or light or heavy cream
1 ½ tablespoons butter, softened
½ teaspoon salt
¼ teaspoon ground white pepper

Taste and adjust the seasonings and cook just until heated through. Serve piping hot. If desired, top with:

Cress Butter, right

CELERY ROOT PUREE

Prepare *Root Vegetable Puree, above,* substituting 2 medium celery roots (about 1 ½ pounds total), peeled, quartered, and thinly sliced, for the carrots. Flavor with a little Dijon mustard and minced fresh thyme or snipped fresh chives.

Cress Butter

About ¼ cup

Wonderfully zippy with root vegetables.
In a small bowl, cream with a fork or wooden spoon:

4 tablespoons (½ stick) butter (preferably unsalted), softened

Gradually stir in:

1 ½ teaspoons finely chopped watercress
Dash of lemon juice
Salt and ground white pepper to taste

Roll the mixture into a cylinder in a piece of wax or parchment paper, plastic wrap, or aluminum foil (or shape as desired), and refrigerate or freeze until firm enough to slice. Or refrigerate in a small bowl or ramekin and spoon on just before serving.

Zucchini Pancakes with Mint and Feta Cheese

About 19 pancakes; 6 to 8 servings

Shred on the large holes of a grater or in a food processor:

2½ pounds green or golden zucchini

Sprinkle lightly with:

Salt

Mix together in a bowl:

2 large eggs

½ cup crumbled feta cheese

½ cup dry unseasoned breadcrumbs

¼ cup all-purpose flour

1 bunch scallions (white part and 2 inches of green), slivered

2 cloves garlic, minced

½ cup chopped fresh parsley

3 tablespoons chopped fresh mint or 1½ tablespoons chopped fresh marjoram

Salt and ground black pepper to taste

Quickly rinse the squash, then, using your hands or a dish towel, squeeze out the excess liquid. Add the squash to the batter. Preheat the oven to 200°F. Heat in a large skillet:

2 tablespoons olive oil

Drop in the batter, using ¼ cup for a 4-inch cake. Fry over medium heat until golden brown on the bottom, about 4 minutes. Turn and brown the second side. Keep the fried pancakes warm in the oven while you fry the remaining batter, adding more oil if needed.

Corn Fritters

4 servings

Corn geneticists have engineered a bundle of sugar-enhanced and super-sweet hybrids that are designed to remain sweet and nonstarchy while shipped and stored for supermarket sales. That is why we now get fresh supermarket corn all winter long. Compared to most summer corn, however, winter corn lacks moisture, creaminess, and tenderness. Summer corn should be used here.

Cut and scrape the kernels from:

5 ears sweet corn (about 2½ cups)

Place the corn and pulp in a large bowl and stir in:

2 large egg yolks, lightly beaten

2 tablespoons all-purpose flour

1 tablespoon sugar

¼ teaspoon salt

⅛ teaspoon ground black pepper

Beat until the peaks are stiff but not dry:

2 large egg whites

Fold the egg whites into the corn mixture. Heat in a large nonstick skillet over high heat until hot:

2 tablespoons butter or vegetable oil

Drop in the batter, a heaping tablespoon at a time. Reduce the heat to medium and cook until browned on the bottom, 2 to 3 minutes. Turn once (do not pat the fritters down) and cook the second side until browned. Take care not to overcook them. Serve immediately.

Potato and Eggplant Curry with Tomato and Fresh Cilantro

4 servings

If you like, replace the eggplant with the same amount of zucchini.

Cut into ¾-inch dice:

1 large eggplant (about 4 cups)

Peel and cut into ½-inch dice:

3 medium boiling potatoes

Chop and reserve the juice from:

One 14½-ounce can whole tomatoes

Heat in a large cast-iron or other heavy skillet over medium-high heat:

3 tablespoons canola oil

Add and stir-fry until lightly browned and fragrant, about 20 seconds:

1 teaspoon cumin seeds

Add and stir-fry for 30 more seconds:

½ teaspoon minced garlic

½ teaspoon grated or minced fresh ginger

¼ teaspoon turmeric

Add the tomatoes (without the juice) to the pan along with:

1 teaspoon sugar

½ teaspoon salt

Cook until most of the liquid is evaporated and the oil begins to separate and pool, about 3 minutes. Add the eggplant, potatoes, and tomato juice. Cover and simmer until the vegetables are tender, about 20 minutes. Stir in:

2 tablespoons fresh lemon juice

2 tablespoons chopped fresh cilantro

1 serrano or jalapeño pepper, finely chopped

Serve with:

Indian or pita bread

Saag Paneer

4 servings

Saag Paneer, which literally translates as "spinach cheese," is a typical Indian vegetarian combination of vegetables and protein, in this case a fresh cheese. Our recipe is a variation on the traditional recipe—the spinach is stir-fried quickly rather than cooked to a puree. Be sure to use a nonstick pan to fry the cheese so it does not stick.

In a medium, heavy saucepan, bring to a boil:

4 cups whole milk

Remove the pan from the heat and add:

3 tablespoons fresh lemon juice

Stir until the milk curdles and separates into bits of solid curd floating in the liquid whey. Let stand for 5 minutes, then pour through a fine-mesh sieve lined with a double layer of cheesecloth. Let stand until cool enough to handle, then pull the corners of the cloth together over the curd and squeeze out as much liquid as possible. Flatten the curd, still in the cheesecloth, to a thickness of ½ to 1 inch. Set it on a plate and top with another plate. Weight with a can and let stand for 20 minutes, then cut the cheese into ½-inch cubes.

Coarsely chop:

Two 10-ounce bunches spinach, stemmed and washed well

Heat in a large nonstick skillet over medium-high heat:

¼ cup canola oil

Add and cook until lightly browned, about 15 seconds:

1 teaspoon cumin seeds

Add the cheese cubes and sauté, shaking the pan every now and then to turn the cubes, until golden brown, 3 to 4 minutes. Remove the cheese and set aside. Add to the oil in the pan:

1 medium onion, thinly sliced

Cook until softened and translucent, 3 to 4 minutes. Add and sauté for 1 minute:

4 cloves garlic, thinly sliced

2 small dried red chili peppers

Add as much chopped spinach as will comfortably fit into the pan, cover, and cook until wilted enough to add more spinach. Add a few more handfuls of spinach, cover, and continue until all the spinach is wilted. Sprinkle with:

½ teaspoon salt

Cook, uncovered, until all the water is evaporated. Fold in the fried cheese, remove the red peppers, and serve hot.

Curried Parsnips

4 to 6 servings

Serve as an entrée over rice or lentils.
Peel, core, and cut into large matchsticks (batons):
1½ pounds parsnips
Drop into a pot of boiling salted water and boil for 2 minutes; drain. Cook in a large skillet over medium heat until softened, about 5 minutes:
3 tablespoons butter or vegetable oil

½ onion, finely diced
Add and cook, stirring constantly, for 1 minute:
1 tablespoon curry powder
Stir in:
½ cup *Vegetable Stock*, 17, or whole milk
Add the parsnips and simmer, covered, over low heat until tender, about 10 minutes. Stir in but do not boil:

½ cup yogurt
Season with:
Salt and ground black pepper to taste
Garnish with:
4 slender scallions (including 2 inches of green), thinly sliced
Fresh cilantro sprigs (optional)

Moroccan-Style Vegetable Stew

6 servings

Serve this wonderful stew over a bed of warm couscous.

Heat in a large Dutch oven:

2 tablespoons butter or olive oil

Add and cook over medium heat for 2 to 3 minutes:

2 medium onions, chopped

Stir in:

1½ cups *Vegetable Stock, 17*

Simmer, stirring often, over medium-low heat until the onions are very tender, about 20 minutes.

Meanwhile, mix in a large bowl:

1 teaspoon ground cumin
¾ teaspoon chili powder
½ teaspoon ground cardamom
½ teaspoon ground cinnamon
½ teaspoon freshly grated or ground nutmeg

Pinch of ground cloves

Stir in:

1 small butternut squash (1½ pounds), peeled, halved, seeded, and cut into ½-inch cubes
1 large Idaho potato (10 ounces), peeled, halved, and cut into ¾-inch pieces

Add the squash mixture to the onions along with:

3 medium carrots, peeled and cut into ¼-inch slices
¼ cup raisins
5 cloves garlic, minced

Bring to a simmer, then reduce the heat to medium-low. Cover first with a sheet of aluminum foil placed directly on the surface of the vegetables, then with the lid. Simmer

gently until the vegetables are completely tender, about 25 minutes. Stir in:

1 or 2 medium zucchini, halved lengthwise, cut into ⅓-inch slices
One 15-ounce can chickpeas, rinsed and drained
⅓ cup halved pitted Kalamata or Niçoise olives
1 teaspoon salt
¼ teaspoon ground black pepper

Simmer, covered, until the zucchini is tender, about 10 minutes. Stir in:

¼ cup chopped fresh parsley or cilantro
3 tablespoons fresh lemon juice
Several drops of hot red pepper sauce

Winter Root Vegetable Braise

4 main-dish servings

Serve this stew in soup plates with pieces of garlic-rubbed toast, or surround it with mashed potatoes. In addition to the vegetables listed, you could also include fennel, salsify, parsley root, artichokes, and Jerusalem artichokes.

Heat in a large skillet or Dutch oven over medium heat:

1½ tablespoons olive oil
1 tablespoon butter
1 bay leaf
1 large sprig fresh thyme

Add:

2 onions, diced

Cook, stirring occasionally, until the onions begin to brown and have left a sugary residue on the bottom of the pan, about 12 minutes. Add and cook for 3 minutes more:

4 large mushrooms, wiped clean and thickly sliced
2 cloves garlic, minced

Pour in:

½ cup dry white wine

Increase the heat and boil, scraping the bottom of the pan, until the liquid is reduced to a syrup, about 5 minutes. Add:

8 ounces turnips, peeled and quartered
8 ounces small rutabagas, peeled and cut into 1-inch cubes
1 pound celery root, peeled and cut into 1-inch cubes

1 tablespoon all-purpose flour
½ teaspoon salt

Stir the vegetables together, then pour in:

2½ cups *Vegetable Stock*, 17

Bring to a boil. Reduce the heat and simmer, covered, until the vegetables are tender, 20 to 25 minutes. Mix together:

3 tablespoons heavy cream
1 tablespoon Dijon mustard

Pour this into the stew and stir well. Season with:

Ground black pepper to taste
Fresh thyme leaves or chopped fresh parsley

Mushroom Ragout

4 servings

Serve over soft polenta, rice, garlic-rubbed croutons, or popovers. For more intense flavor, soak ½ ounce dried mushrooms, chop, and add with the fresh mushrooms; use the soaking water for part of the liquid.

Heat over medium-high heat in a large saucepan:

1 tablespoon olive oil

Add and cook until golden, about 10 minutes:

1 onion, diced

Remove and set aside. Heat in the same pan over medium heat:

1 tablespoon olive oil

Add and cook until they begin to release their liquid:

1 pound assorted fresh mushrooms, wiped clean and thickly sliced

Add the onions along with:

2 cloves garlic, finely chopped
1 teaspoon chopped fresh rosemary, or scant ½ teaspoon dried
Salt and cracked black peppercorns to taste

Cook until the mushrooms begin to brown, another 3 to 4 minutes. Stir in:

1 tablespoon tomato paste

Increase the heat to high and cook, stirring, for 1 to 2 minutes more. Add:

1½ cups *Vegetable Stock*, 17

Reduce the heat and simmer for 10 minutes. Stir in to form a sauce:

2 tablespoons cold butter, cut into pieces
1½ teaspoons balsamic vinegar

Garnish with:

Grated Parmesan cheese (optional)
Chopped fresh parsley

MUSHROOMS

These days, you can find a variety of mushrooms at the supermarket. Porcini, also called cèpes or boletes, look like very large button mushrooms with thick stalks and reddish caps. They are among the tastiest of wild mushrooms. Chanterelles, or girolles, resemble a curving trumpet. Their golden or orange-brown caps and slender stems can hint of apricots or be delicately earthy. Creminis, or Italian browns, are the same as common button mushrooms, only grown outdoors and bigger. Oyster mushrooms have small fan-shaped caps with short stems, cream colored to grayish brown. Their texture is smooth, and their flavor can have a touch of the sea.

Greek Spinach and Cheese Pie (Spanakopita)

About thirty 2-inch squares or diamonds

Stem, wash well, and coarsely chop:

2 pounds (or three 10-ounce bags) spinach

Heat in a large skillet over medium heat:

2 tablespoons olive oil

Add and cook until softened, 5 to 7 minutes:

1 large onion, finely chopped
4 scallions, finely chopped

Add the chopped spinach a handful at a time. Cook until the spinach is wilted and the liquid is released, 5 minutes. Increase the heat to high and cook, stirring often, until the liquid is evaporated and the spinach is dry, 7 to 10 minutes. Stir in:

¼ cup snipped fresh dill or chopped fresh parsley

Let stand until cool enough to handle, then squeeze to remove the excess liquid. In a medium bowl, lightly beat:

4 large eggs

Add the cooked spinach mixture along with:

8 ounces feta cheese, crumbled
2 tablespoons grated kefalotiri (Greek grating cheese) or Parmesan cheese
½ teaspoon salt
Several grinds of black pepper
Pinch of freshly grated or ground nutmeg

Lightly oil a 13 x 9-inch baking pan. Melt:

8 tablespoons (1 stick) butter

Unroll on a dry work surface:

1 pound phyllo dough, thawed if frozen

Trim 1 inch from the edges of the phyllo dough. Cover with plastic wrap and cover the plastic with a damp towel. Lay 1 sheet of phyllo in and up the sides of the prepared pan and brush lightly with melted butter. Top with 7 more phyllo sheets, brushing each one lightly with butter. Spread the spinach mixture over the layered phyllo. Top with 8 more sheets, brushing each one with butter, including the top sheet. Roll the overhanging phyllo from the sides to form a border all the way around. With a thin, sharp knife, cut the pie into squares or diamonds, but do not cut through the bottom or the filling will leak onto the pan. Refrigerate for 30 minutes. Preheat the oven to 375°F. Bake the spinach pie until crisp and golden, about 45 minutes. Remove from the oven and let stand for a few minutes. Cut the squares or diamonds right through to the bottom and serve.

WORKING WITH PHYLLO

Phyllo, literally *leaf* in Greek, is available frozen in most grocery stores or fresh from Greek and Middle Eastern bakeries. It is essential to keep the thin sheets from drying out. If using frozen phyllo, thaw it slowly, without unwrapping, in the refrigerator for several hours or overnight. Once it is thawed, unwrap the phyllo and remove only the number of sheets required for the recipe; rewrap the remaining sheets in plastic wrap and return to the refrigerator or freezer.

Red Peppers Stuffed with Saffron Rice and Pine Nuts

4 to 6 servings

Halve lengthwise, keeping the stems intact, and seed:

2 large or 3 medium red bell peppers

Steam over boiling water until slightly softened, 8 to 10 minutes. Heat in a wide saucepan:

2 tablespoons olive oil

Add and cook over medium heat until softened:

6 scallions (white part and 1 inch of green), chopped

3 cloves garlic, minced

⅛ teaspoon crushed saffron threads

Add and stir briefly to coat with oil:

1½ cups long-grain white rice

Add and bring to a boil:

1¾ cups water or *Vegetable Stock*, 17

Stir, reduce the heat to low, and cover. Cook for 10 minutes, then let stand, covered, for 10 minutes more. Preheat the oven to 350°F.

Fluff the rice, turn it into a large bowl to cool, then add:

2 cups shredded provolone cheese

⅓ cup pine nuts, toasted

¼ cup chopped fresh parsley

2 tablespoons chopped fresh marjoram or basil

Mix well and season with:

Salt and ground black pepper to taste

Place the peppers in a baking dish in which they fit snugly. Spoon the filling into each pepper half, mounding the top. Add to the bottom of the dish:

½ cup water

Cover lightly with aluminum foil and bake until heated through, about 35 minutes. Serve sprinkled with:

Chopped fresh parsley

Summer Squash Gratin

6 servings

This crumbly, golden gratin is irresistible. Try it with pattypan or straightneck squash. Pattypan or scallop squash are flattened rounds with scalloped edges, picked 3 inches wide or less. Their flavor is lighter and nuttier than zucchini. Heritage pattypans are pale green. Hybrids are more rounded and can be gold or dark green. Straightneck squash have the same flavor as pattypan but look like yellow zucchini.

Preheat the oven to 350°F. Lightly butter a 10-inch gratin dish.

Steam until tender, about 10 minutes:

1¼ pounds yellow squash, cut into ½-inch cubes

Remove to a medium bowl. Cook in a small skillet until softened:

1 tablespoon butter or olive oil
½ small onion, finely diced

Add to the squash along with:

⅔ cup diced Monterey Jack, raclette, Swiss, or Teleme cheese
⅓ cup crème fraîche
2 tablespoons grated Parmesan cheese
1 tablespoon white vermouth or dry white wine
1 teaspoon ground coriander
Salt and ground white pepper to taste

Pour into the prepared dish. Combine and sprinkle over the top:

½ cup fresh breadcrumbs
1 tablespoon melted butter

Bake until bubbling and golden, about 35 minutes.

Kale and Potato Gratin

6 servings

Kale deserves to be appreciated as much as spinach. Its crisp, curled, crinkly, or deeply cut leaves have a rich but delicate cabbage taste and hold their texture in cooking.

Preheat the oven to 350°F. Butter a 2-quart gratin dish.

Have ready:

4 medium Yukon gold or all-purpose potatoes (about 1¼ pounds), peeled and cut into ⅛-inch-thick rounds
2 small onions, cut into ⅛-inch-thick slices

Steam until almost tender, 8 to 10 minutes:

1 large bunch (about 1 pound) kale, stemmed and washed

Drain and let stand until cool enough to handle. Press out the excess water and coarsely chop. In the gratin dish, build up alternating layers of potatoes, onions, and kale, beginning and ending with the potatoes. Dot each onion layer with:

1 tablespoon butter, cut into pieces
½ teaspoon minced fresh tarragon
¼ teaspoon salt
⅛ teaspoon ground black pepper

Pour over the layers:

1½ cups milk or half-and-half

Cover and bake until the potatoes are tender and almost all the liquid is absorbed, 30 to 45 minutes. Broil, if desired, to brown the top. Serve.

Rolled Stuffed Eggplants

4 servings

A great summer entrée. The rolls can be formed well in advance and refrigerated before baking.

Preheat the oven to 400°F. Lightly oil a 13 x 9-inch baking dish.

Combine in a bowl:

¾ cup shredded provolone or mozzarella cheese

¾ cup ricotta cheese

2 tablespoons grated Parmesan cheese

2 tablespoons chopped fresh marjoram or basil

1 small clove garlic, minced

Cut lengthwise into ¼-inch-thick slices:

1 large eggplant (about 1¼ pounds)

Brush both sides of the slices with:

Olive oil

Cook the eggplant in batches in a skillet until golden, about 5 minutes each side, then remove to a platter. Spread a mound of the cheese mixture at the base of each eggplant slice, then roll it up. Arrange the rolls seam side down in the baking dish. Cover the dish and bake until heated through and the cheese is melted, about 20 minutes. Remove the rolls to warmed plates. Serve surrounded with:

Italian Tomato Sauce, 46

Vegetable Potpie with Cheddar Biscuit Crust

8 to 12 servings

This dish can be prepared up to 1 day ahead: Cut up, brown, and place the vegetables in the baking dish. The crust can be made up to 2 hours ahead and kept covered at room temperature. Keep the vegetables in large chunks so that they remain intact and do not cook down to a puree.

Prepare and keep each vegetable in separate bowls:

2 medium red onions (about 1 pound), cut into thick slices

3 medium carrots, peeled and cut into 1-inch pieces

3 parsnips, peeled and cut into 1-inch pieces

1 celery root, peeled and cut into 1-inch pieces

1 butternut squash (about 2½ pounds), peeled and cut into 1-inch pieces

1 acorn squash (about 1½ pounds), peeled and cut into 1-inch pieces

8 ounces portobello mushrooms, cut into thick slices and slices halved crosswise

Have ready:

3 or 4 tablespoons olive oil

3 or 4 tablespoons unsalted butter

Heat ½ tablespoon oil and ½ tablespoon butter in a large skillet over medium-high heat. Add the onion slices and cook until browned, about 3 minutes on each side. Transfer to a large bowl and season with:

Salt and ground black pepper to taste

Add a bit more oil and butter to the pan, then add the carrots and parsnips. Brown, stirring frequently, for 5 to 7 minutes, transfer to the bowl, and season with salt and pepper. Repeat, adding oil and butter as needed, with the celery root and squashes, browning them all separately and seasoning with salt and pepper as you place them in the bowl. Finally, add the mushrooms to the pan with more oil and butter if needed, turn the heat to high, and brown them well, tossing frequently, about 5 to 7 minutes. Add to the bowl and season with salt and pepper. Preheat the oven to 400°F.

Add to the vegetables:

2 tablespoons chopped fresh marjoram, or 1 tablespoon dried

Gently mix the herb and vegetables together, transfer to a 13 x 9-inch baking dish, and spread evenly in 1 layer. Pour over the vegetables:

4 cups *Vegetable Stock*, 17

Cover the dish and bake until the vegetables are just tender when pierced with the tip of a sharp knife, 30 to 45 minutes. While the vegetables bake, prepare the biscuit crust. Whisk together thoroughly in a large bowl:

2 cups all-purpose flour

2½ teaspoons baking powder

½ to ¾ teaspoon salt

Drop in:

5 to 6 tablespoons cold unsalted butter, cut into pieces

Cut in the butter with 2 knives or a pastry blender, tossing the pieces with the flour mixture to coat and separate them as you work. For biscuits with crunchy edges and a flaky, layered structure, continue to cut in the butter until the largest pieces are the size of peas and the rest resemble breadcrumbs. For classic fluffy biscuits, continue to cut in the butter until the mixture resembles coarse breadcrumbs. Do not allow the butter to melt or form a paste with the flour.

Add all at once:

¾ cup heavy cream

¾ cup grated Cheddar cheese

2 teaspoons minced garlic (optional)

¼ teaspoon cracked black pepper

Mix with a rubber spatula, wooden spoon, or fork just until most of the dry ingredients are moistened. With a lightly floured hand, gather the dough into a ball and knead it gently against the sides and bottom of the bowl 5 to 10 times, turning and pressing any loose pieces into the dough each time until they adhere and the bowl is fairly clean. Set aside. After the vegetables have cooked for 30 to 45 minutes, uncover the dish and spoon dollops of biscuit dough over the vegetables. Continue baking until the biscuits are browned, 20 to 25 minutes more. Remove from the oven, let stand for 10 minutes, and serve.

CELERY ROOT

More or less round, it has a daunting appearance–knobby, grimy, and perhaps tangled at the roots. But beneath the skin is tender, cream-colored flesh with a nutty taste. An autumn and winter vegetable, it is also called celeriac and turnip-root celery. Select small to medium knobs, the heaviest for their size. They should have no cuts, bruises, or soft spots. If there are stalks on top, they should be crisp and fresh. You can use the stalks for seasoning–they have the concentrated flavor of Chinese celery.

Tuscan-Style Stuffed Artichokes

6 appetizer servings

Preheat the oven to 375°F.

Trim as directed below:

6 medium artichokes

To prevent discoloration, rub all the cut surfaces with:

½ lemon

Combine well:

6 tablespoons extra-virgin olive oil

6 tablespoons fresh breadcrumbs, toasted

¼ cup minced fresh parsley

3 cloves garlic, minced

3 tablespoons grated Parmesan cheese

Salt and ground black pepper to taste

Using a teaspoon, fill the cavities of the artichokes with this mixture. Place the stuffed artichokes in a baking dish in which they fit snugly.

Pour ½ inch of water into the bottom of the dish and add to it:

Juice of ½ lemon

1 tablespoon extra-virgin olive oil

Cover the dish with aluminum foil and bake until the artichokes are tender, about 45 minutes. Serve warm or at room temperature.

HOW TO PREPARE ARTICHOKES

Have on hand a lemon half or two; its juice rubbed over cut surfaces keeps the flesh from discoloring.

1 Use scissors to trim off the tough, thorny tops of the outside layers of leaves. Bend each leaf back and snap off the top, or snip it off with scissors—the only method that works with tough end-of-the-season artichokes. Rub cut surfaces frequently with lemon.

2 When you reach the thin inner leaves that are green at the top but celery yellow at the base, lay the artichokes on their sides on a cutting board. With a sharp, heavy, stainless-steel knife or a serrated knife, trim off the top inch or so of the inner leaves.

3 Pull out the immature prickly, pinkish leaves in the center.

4 Use the tip of a spoon to scrape up the thicket of fuzz beneath, called the choke. It will lift up in small pieces. Be careful not to cut into the heart.

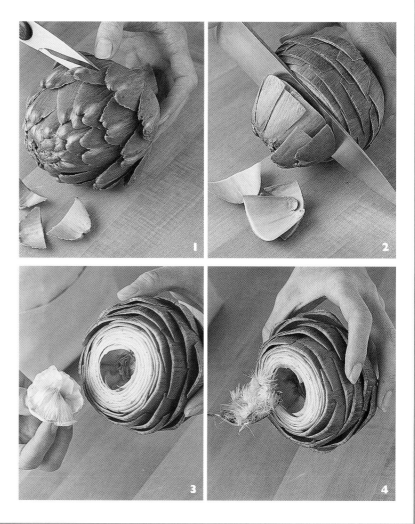

Garlic-Braised Broccoli Rabe or Rapini

4 servings

Broccoli rabe's leaves and buds are mustardy but sweet; it is an autumn green. Rapini, a springtime green, is another mostly leafy plant and is often confused with broccoli rabe. Rapini leaves and buds have a mustardy bite, much like turnip greens, which they resemble.

Bring to a rolling boil in a stockpot:

16 cups (4 quarts) water

1½ tablespoons salt

Thinly slice the greens, peel the stems, and cut into 1-inch pieces:

1 bunch broccoli rabe or rapini (about 1 pound)

Boil for 2 minutes, then drain and squeeze the moisture out of the leaves. Heat in a large skillet over medium heat:

2 tablespoons extra-virgin olive oil

Add:

1 clove garlic, thinly sliced

1 small dried red chili pepper (optional)

Add the broccoli rabe and cook over medium heat until tender, about 4 minutes. Remove the chili pepper and season with:

Salt and ground black pepper to taste

Serve hot.

June Vegetable Ragout

4 servings

You can substitute four 9-ounce packages of frozen artichoke hearts, thawed and quartered, for the fresh artichokes in this recipe. It is worth it, though, to make this dish with fresh artichokes.

Trim and quarter:

8 large artichoke hearts, or 16 baby artichokes

As you work, drop them into a bowl of water with lemon juice added. Cut lengthwise in half and peel:

2 medium onions

Place each half, cut side down, on a cutting board and cut crosswise into very thin slices. In an unheated large skillet, combine the onions with:

6 tablespoons extra-virgin olive oil

1 plump head garlic, separated into cloves and peeled, cloves halved lengthwise

1 small bunch summer savory or stems and sprigs of thyme and parsley, tied with kitchen string

Salt to taste

Toss to coat the ingredients with the oil. Cover and sweat over low heat until the onions are softened, about 10 minutes. Drain and add the artichokes and:

2 pounds fava beans, blanched, refreshed, and shelled

3 tomatoes, peeled, seeded, and coarsely chopped

1½ cups dry white wine

Simmer, uncovered, for 10 minutes to evaporate the alcohol. Add:

2 pounds fresh peas in their pods, shelled, blanched, and refreshed (about 2 cups)

20 asparagus tips, blanched and refreshed

Cook until the green vegetables are heated through, about 2 minutes more. Remove the pan from the heat and immediately stir in until creamy:

2 tablespoons cold unsalted butter, cut into small pieces

Remove and discard the bundle of savory. Taste for seasoning. Serve immediately with crusty bread.

ABOUT
BEANS
& TOFU

*A*n excellent source of protein, vitamins, minerals, and fiber, beans are what nutritionists like to call a "powerhouse"—a food that is unusually rich in nutrients but relatively low in calories. Because they are digested slowly, and thus raise blood sugar very gently, they are sometimes recommended for diabetics. Their high fiber content, both water soluble and nonsoluble, has been linked to lower blood cholesterol. And it is suspected that beans contain some compounds that protect against cancers.

Tofu is the humble soybean's leap toward culinary art, especially in the cuisines of China, where it was invented more than a thousand years ago, and Japan. Tofu (also called bean curd and dofu) is made like cheese, by coagulating soy milk until it forms curds, which are broken up and then pressed. But tofu is unlike cheese in that it rarely stands on its own. Instead, it bathes in the flavors of sauces, marinades, and dressings. Its smoothness can range from as soft as custard to as chewy as a bread dumpling. A 4-ounce serving provides up to one-quarter of a day's protein requirement, about 10 grams of fat, and no cholesterol. Since most tofu is coagulated with a calcium compound, it also provides a goodly amount of that mineral.

Red Bean and Lima Succotash, 82

Soaking and Cooking Beans

Whether or not to soak beans before cooking is a hot topic today. Many noted food professionals, whose opinions we hold in high regard, argue that fresh dried beans do not benefit from presoaking before cooking. Heating the legumes to boiling and then simmering them until they swell with water and soften can be done in one continuous process. In order to ensure success with this method, the beans must be of high quality and fresh. Given the limited availability of high-quality fresh beans, presoaking the beans first is kinder, both to the bean and to the cook. Not only does it save anywhere from 30 minutes to over an hour on the stove, but it also treats the seed coat more gently than steady simmering, so that the shape of the bean holds without breaking. At high elevations, where simmering times will be extended by the lower temperature of the boiling water, soaking for up to 24 hours is good time-saving insurance.

Before you prepare any legumes, spread them in a pan or large colander and remove any tiny stones that may have accompanied them out of the field. Then rinse the beans very well under cold water, raking them with your fingers to get rid of any clumps of dirt.

Our preferred soaking method is to heat the soaking water, which hastens the swelling of the beans. For a gentle quick-soak, pour boiling water over the beans to cover by 2 inches, cover, let stand until the beans have swelled to at least twice their size and have absorbed most of the water, and then drain, discarding the soaking liquid. This will take at least an hour and possibly longer, but the beans will remain firm and keep their shape when cooked.

Another way to soak beans is to place them in a large bowl or pot and add water to cover by at least 2 inches. Cover and let stand for up to 24 hours; refrigerate to prevent fermentation if the kitchen is very warm. The beans will swell to triple their dried size. Drain well and discard the soaking liquid.

A third method, which risks breaking some bean skins, is to place the beans in a saucepan, add water to cover by 2 inches, and heat to boiling; then reduce the heat and simmer for 2 minutes. Let stand, covered, for 1 hour. Or microwave 1 pound beans and 4 cups water in a covered 3- to 4-quart casserole on high to boiling, 12 to 17 minutes, and then on medium for 2 minutes. Stir and let stand, covered, for 1 hour. With all three soaking methods, be sure to rinse and drain the beans before the final cooking.

To cook, place beans in a large pot and add cold water to cover by 2 inches. Bring to a boil over high heat; skim off the foam that rises to the surface. Reduce the heat to low and cover; simmer, stirring and skimming occasionally, until the beans are tender. Do not boil rapidly or the abrasion will loosen the bean skins. If the pot threatens to boil over, partially remove the cover.

Beans readily absorb seasonings from water. Simmer beans with chopped onions and carrots to sweeten them; use at least a cup of each with a pound of beans, because the water will dilute their impact.

If you want relatively firm beans, for a salad or side dish or to use in recipes that call for further cooking without acidic ingredients, remove a few beans and pinch them for tenderness at the low end of the cooking time range suggested in the recipe. If you want very soft beans for a soup, you may decide to cook them longer than suggested.

SUBSTITUTING CANNED BEANS

Canned beans can be substituted cup for cup in recipes that call for cooked beans, but they are almost always softer and less flavorful. Since brands vary in quality, it is worth trying different ones. When choosing canned beans, certain varieties hold up better during the canning process than others. White beans seem to stand up less well to canning than, for example, chickpeas. Rinsing canned beans improves the taste a little and removes excess salt.

HOW TO SPROUT BEANS

To make 1½ cups sprouts, start with 3 tablespoons dried beans. Seeds, such as alfalfa, wheat, and radish, can be sprouted the same way.

1 Pick over and rinse beans. Place in a large bowl and cover with about 2 inches warm (not hot) water. Let stand for up to 24 hours; drain and rinse.

2 Place the beans in a sterile 1-quart glass jar. Cover with a double layer of cheesecloth (or a finer-weave cloth if sprouting very small seeds) and secure with a rubber band.

3 Twice a day, fill the jar with cool water and drain it off through the cheesecloth. Be sure to drain well to avoid inviting mold.

4 Pale shoots should appear within 5 days and are ready to harvest when about 1 inch long. Before harvesting, place the jar in the sun for a few hours to encourage the shoots to produce chlorophyll. Discard beans that do not sprout.

Sprouting Beans

The most fundamental bean transformation is sprouting, or turning the bean and its embryo into the beginnings of a plant. Almost all organically grown beans, if not too old, can be sprouted, but do not sprout fava beans, for there may be some risk in eating these raw. Lentils and adzuki and mung beans, those that make the threadlike sprouts commonly used in Chinese cooking, are good choices, because small beans tend to sprout more readily than large ones. Small amounts of sprouts can be eaten raw—in a sandwich or sprinkled over a salad, for example—but if you are using more than a large handful, heat them briefly to improve digestibility. You can add them toward the end of cooking to other vegetables, grains, and stir-fries.

The vivid variety of sprouted legumes available—more bean than sprout in most cases—make good snacks and salad ingredients. They also contribute texture and color to rice; add them, without stirring, for the last few minutes of cooking.

Tofu

Tofu is as perishable as dairy foods and highly susceptible to bacterial contamination, so wash your hands and work surfaces and keep the tofu refrigerated as you would milk and cheese. When buying refrigerated tofu, check the expiration date. You can leave it in its tub or pouch, but it is better to open the package, discard the liquid, and pour in fresh water; change the water daily. It will keep this way for up to a week, depending on its freshness when purchased. Because of the risk of contamination, it is best to avoid tofu sold from open tubs, even if it is refrigerated.

The tofu called "silken," often sold in aseptic boxes, is labeled soft or firm, but either one is much more fragile than regular tofu. Made more like yogurt than like cheese, silken tofu is coagulated from thick soy milk and not pressed.

The tofu used for cooking, sometimes called "cotton" tofu, is labeled soft, firm, or extra firm, depending on how much liquid was drained off during processing. Firm and extra firm hold together better in the pot. Cooks commonly firm up tofu by pressing it under a weight for 30 to 60 minutes, depending on how much water the tofu starts out with and the desired firmness.

HOW TO PRESS TOFU

1 To press a 1-pound block of tofu, cut it horizontally in half to make two slabs, each about 1 inch thick.

2 Place a sheet of aluminum foil over a cutting board large enough to hold both slabs side by side. To allow the water to drain off, place one end of the board over the edge of the sink or on a baking sheet and prop up the other end with a ¼-cup measure or an inch-thick box.

3 Place the tofu on the board and cover with another sheet of foil. Place a second cutting board or similarly shaped weight over the tofu and let stand for 10 minutes to compact somewhat. The sides of the tofu should bulge very slightly, but be careful not to overweight soft tofu before it has compacted, or it may split. After 10 minutes, add more weight, evenly distributed; a cast-iron skillet or Dutch oven with two or three large cans in it, several nested heavy skillets, or several large books will do the job. Check the weighted tofu for firmness after 30 minutes; if desired, turn the slabs over, replace the weight, and press for an additional 15 to 30 minutes. Refrigerate pressed tofu in a bowl of water; it will not reabsorb water and can be kept for 2 to 3 days if you change the water daily. This extra step is not essential, just a textural refinement.

Classic Black Beans (Frijoles Negros)

6 servings

These are delicious served with nothing more than a spoonful of sour cream or yogurt and some diced avocados, but they are also very good served in warm tortillas or as a soup garnished with cilantro leaves. Pinto, pink, kidney, and navy beans can be substituted for the black beans.

Pick over and rinse:

1 pound dried black beans (about 2½ cups)

Drain. Heat in a large saucepan over medium heat:

3 tablespoons vegetable oil

Add:

1 medium onion, diced

Cook, stirring often, until deep golden brown, about 10 minutes. Stir in the beans along with:

8 cups water

1 large sprig fresh epazote (optional)

1 fresh jalapeño pepper or dried chipotle pepper, halved and seeded (optional)

Remove any beans that float. Bring to a boil. Reduce the heat to medium-low and simmer, partially covered, until the beans are thoroughly tender, about 1 hour. Stir the beans regularly and add water as needed to keep the liquid a generous ½ inch above the level of the beans.

Season with:

Salt and ground black pepper to taste

Simmer for another 10 to 15 minutes for the beans to absorb the seasoning, then remove from the heat. Serve hot.

Refried Beans

6 servings

A classic Mexican side dish. The beans are easier to mash if they are warm.

Heat in a large skillet over medium-high heat:

2 tablespoons vegetable oil

Add:

1 medium white onion, chopped

Cook, stirring often, until deep golden brown, about 10 minutes. Add:

4 cloves garlic, minced

Cook, stirring, for 1 minute. Add with a slotted spoon 1 cup at a time:

4 cups undrained *Classic Black Beans, above,* or cooked black beans (about 1⅓ cups dried), undrained if canned

Mash each addition of beans to a coarse puree with a potato masher or the back of a large spoon before adding the next cupful. Stir in:

1 cup cooking liquid or water

Cook, stirring often, over medium to low heat until the beans are a little soupier than you would like to serve them—they will thicken as they sit. The whole mashing and cooking process will take 10 to 15 minutes.

Season with:

Salt to taste

Serve warm with:

Crumbled queso fresco, feta, or grated Parmesan cheese

Tortilla chips

Vegetarian Chili

8 servings

A delicious "warmer upper" (opposite). Heat in a large saucepan over medium heat:

2 tablespoons olive oil

Add:

1 cup chopped peeled carrots
1 cup chopped red bell peppers
1 cup chopped green bell peppers
1 cup chopped onions
2 cloves garlic, minced

Cook, stirring, until the onions are golden, 12 to 15 minutes. Add:

1 to 2 fresh green chili peppers, seeded and finely chopped, or 1 chipotle pepper in adobo sauce, minced
1 tablespoon ground ancho chili pepper
1 tablespoon ground cumin

Cook, stirring, for 2 minutes. Stir in:

One 28-ounce can plum tomatoes, with juice, coarsely chopped
One 16-ounce can red kidney beans, rinsed and drained, or 1½ cups cooked (about ½ cup dried)
One 16-ounce can cannellini beans, rinsed and drained, or 1½ cups cooked (about ½ cup dried)
One 16-ounce can black beans, rinsed and drained, or 1½ cups cooked (about ½ cup dried)
1 cup tomato juice
Salt to taste

Bring to a boil. Reduce the heat to medium-low and simmer, uncovered, stirring occasionally, until the flavors are blended, adding more tomato juice or water as needed, about 45 minutes. Season and serve with:

Sour cream
***Salsa Fresca*, right**
Chopped fresh cilantro

Red Bean and Lima Succotash

4 servings

The most popular form of succotash combines corn with lima beans—but red kidney or cranberry beans work too. Pick over, rinse, and soak, 78:

½ cup dried red kidney or cranberry beans

Drain. Combine in a medium saucepan with water to cover by 2 inches. Bring to a boil. Reduce the heat and simmer, covered, until the beans are very tender, about 1½ hours. Add water as needed to keep the beans moist. Drain. Bring to a boil in a large saucepan:

1 cup heavy cream

Boil over medium heat until reduced to about ½ cup, being careful not to let it overflow. Add the cooked beans along with:

1½ cups fresh, canned, or frozen corn kernels
1 cup cooked fresh or frozen baby lima beans

Cover and cook over low heat for 10 minutes. Stir in:

1 tablespoon butter
1 teaspoon fresh thyme leaves (optional)
½ teaspoon salt
⅛ teaspoon ground black pepper

Taste and adjust the seasonings. Serve hot.

Salsa Fresca

About 2 cups

This recipe for Mexican salsa is easily doubled or tripled, but try to make only as much as you will use immediately, as it loses its texture on standing and the chili peppers increase in heat. Regional variations include using scallions or white or red onions, water instead of lime juice, and in Yucatán, sour-orange juice instead of lime juice. Any sort of fresh chili pepper can be used. Rinsing the chopped onions eliminates the biting aftertaste that could otherwise overwhelm the other ingredients.

Combine in a medium bowl:

½ small white or red onion or 8 slender scallions, finely chopped, rinsed, and drained
2 tablespoons fresh lime juice or cold water

Prepare the following ingredients, setting them aside, then add all together to the onion mixture:

2 large ripe tomatoes, or 3 to 5 ripe plum tomatoes, seeded, if desired, and finely diced
¼ to ½ cup chopped fresh cilantro (leaves and tender stems)
3 to 5 serrano or fresh jalapeño peppers, or ¼ to 1 habanero pepper, or to taste, seeded and minced
6 radishes, finely diced (optional)
1 medium clove garlic, minced (optional)

Stir together well. Season with:

¼ teaspoon salt, or to taste
Serve immediately.

Couscous with Chickpeas

4 servings

Heat in a large skillet over medium heat:

3 tablespoons olive oil

Add:

1 cup sliced blanched almonds

Cook, stirring, just until lightly golden, 2 to 3 minutes. Add:

3 cloves garlic, finely chopped

Cook, stirring, for about 1 minute. Stir in:

1 teaspoon sweet or hot paprika

1 teaspoon ground cumin

1 teaspoon ground coriander

½ to 1 teaspoon hot red pepper sauce

Cook until heated through, about 1 minute more. Stir in:

2½ cups *Vegetable Stock*, 17, or water

2 cups cooked chickpeas (about ⅔ cup dried), rinsed and drained if canned

1 cup chopped raisins

Bring to a boil and stir in:

1¼ cups quick-cooking couscous

Cover, remove from the heat, and let stand for 5 minutes. Fluff the couscous with a fork. Season with:

Salt and ground black pepper to taste

Garnish with:

¼ cup chopped fresh parsley or cilantro

Curried Chickpeas with Vegetables

4 servings

This makes a perfect entrée.

Heat in a large skillet over medium heat until sizzling:

¼ cup vegetable oil

2 teaspoons cumin seeds

Add:

1 tablespoon minced peeled fresh ginger

1 tablespoon minced garlic

Cook, stirring, over low heat for 1 minute; do not brown. Stir in:

2 teaspoons curry powder

Cook for 1 minute. Stir in:

1¾ cups cooked chickpeas (about ⅔ cup dried), rinsed and drained if canned

2 cups ½-inch cubes peeled sweet potatoes

2 cups cauliflower florets

1 cup 1-inch pieces green beans

1 cup *Vegetable Stock*, 17

½ to 1 teaspoon salt

Ground black pepper to taste

Cover and cook over medium heat until the vegetables are tender, about 10 minutes. Stir together:

1 cup yogurt

2 tablespoons all-purpose flour

Add to the vegetables along with:

1 tablespoon finely chopped fresh jalapeño peppers

Cook, stirring, over low heat until heated through; do not boil. Toast in another skillet over medium-low heat:

2 tablespoons shredded dried coconut, preferably unsweetened

Sprinkle over the vegetables. Top with:

¼ cup chopped roasted unsalted cashews or peanuts

CHICKPEAS

Chickpeas seem indestructible. They come out of a can firmer than other beans, hold up well in stews and salads, and can withstand grinding to make *Falafel*, 44, or baking for a pop-in-your-mouth snack. They are also known as garbanzos and ceci beans; a smaller variety is sold skinless and split as *chana dal* in Indian groceries and can be used instead of split peas to make *Dal, opposite*. Chickpeas are a constant in Mediterranean cuisines, from Middle Eastern hummus to Moroccan couscous, imparting a mild nutty flavor to all.

Classic Tuscan Beans

6 to 8 servings

Tuscans love beans so much that the rest of Italy calls them mangia fagioli, *"the bean eaters." Tradition and goodness come together in this simplest of cooking methods—simmering dried beans seasoned with fresh sage, garlic, and olive oil. Dried cannellini beans are a first choice for their sweet, creamy character. More readily available pinto or cranberry beans come close. Serve hot or at room temperature, drizzling on a thread of olive oil at the table.*

Pick over, rinse, and soak, 78:

1 pound dried cannellini, pinto, or cranberry beans (about 2 cups)

Drain. Combine in a large pot with:

12 fresh sage leaves or whole dried sage leaves

3 cloves garlic, halved

1 tablespoon extra-virgin olive oil

Add water to cover by 3 inches. Bring to a simmer, partially cover, and simmer gently until tender, about 1 hour. Drain. Season to taste with:

Salt and ground black pepper

Serve hot, warm, or at room temperature, seasoning each portion with about:

1 teaspoon extra-virgin olive oil, preferably Tuscan

Indian Lentil Puree (Dal)

4 to 6 servings

Dal is the Hindi word for both an array of legumes used in Indian cooking and a preparation of legumes that is a staple of Indian cuisine. In Indian households where meat is either too expensive or prohibited by religion, dal is likely to be on the table at every meal as the protein. If the dal is pureed, it is soupy or "wet" and eaten with rice; if not pureed, the dal is "dry" and eaten with bread. A pureed dal may be thick or thin, as the cook chooses.

Pick over, rinse, and place in a large saucepan:

1 cup yellow split peas or red lentils

Add:

2 cups water

1 small onion, sliced

¾ teaspoon minced garlic

¾ teaspoon minced peeled fresh ginger

½ teaspoon ground turmeric

Simmer, covered, until the split peas are tender, 20 to 25 minutes. Puree through a food mill and return to the saucepan. Stir in:

1 cup water

¾ teaspoon salt

Simmer, partially covered, until the dal is thickened to the consistency of split pea soup, about 20 minutes. Stir in:

2 fresh serrano or jalapeño peppers, seeded and cut into thirds

1 plum tomato, diced

2 tablespoons chopped fresh cilantro

Serve with:

Hot cooked rice

LENTILS

Whole lentils are thin skinned, require no soaking, and cook relatively quickly. The olive-drab lentils sold everywhere are sometimes called green, other times brown, and are actually shades of both. French green lentils (Le Puy are the finest example) are about half the size of the more common lentils, are much darker green, and have a deeper flavor. Beluga lentils are tiny and black like caviar and deeply flavored; they cook in about half the time of other lentils, hold their shape, and offer a novel appearance. More colorful and very quick cooking are red and yellow lentils; both are skinless and, whether whole or split, dissolve into a puree as they cook.

Sesame Stir-Fried Lentils and Vegetables

4 to 6 servings

Lentils are used in this recipe much as plain cooked rice would be used in fried rice or in a skillet dish of rice heated with vegetables. Serve over rice for an entrée.

Toast in a small skillet over medium heat for about 1 minute:

1 tablespoon sesame seeds

Place in a vegetable steaming basket over boiling water:

1 cup diagonally sliced peeled carrots

2 cups broccoli florets

1 cup halved pattypan squash

1 cup trimmed snow peas

Cover and steam until crisp-tender, about 5 minutes. Rinse with cool water to stop the cooking. Heat in a large skillet over medium-high heat:

2 tablespoons vegetable oil

Add:

½ cup ½-inch pieces red bell peppers

Cook, stirring, for about 2 minutes. Add:

1 tablespoon finely chopped garlic

1 tablespoon finely chopped peeled fresh ginger

¼ teaspoon red pepper flakes (optional)

Cook, stirring, until sizzling, about 30 seconds. Add the steamed vegetables along with:

3 cups cooked brown or green lentils (about 1 cup dried)

½ cup thinly sliced scallions

3 tablespoons light or dark soy sauce

2 teaspoons toasted sesame oil

Cook, stirring, just until heated through, about 3 minutes. Sprinkle with the toasted sesame seeds. Serve hot.

Szechuan Spiced Tofu

4 servings

Vary the hotness of this dish by adjusting the amount of chili paste. As with all stir-fries, have all the ingredients measured, chopped, and ready before beginning to cook.

Heat in a wok or large skillet over medium-high heat:

1 tablespoon peanut or vegetable oil

Add:

2 teaspoons minced peeled fresh ginger

1 teaspoon minced garlic

Stir-fry for 1 minute. Add:

One 8-ounce can flower-cut baby corn, drained

4 cups ½-inch-thick slices bok choy

½ small onion, sliced

Stir-fry until the bok choy is slightly wilted, 3 to 4 minutes. Combine and stir in:

½ cup *Vegetable Stock*, 17

2 tablespoons light or dark soy sauce

1 tablespoon black bean sauce or black bean paste

1 tablespoon dry sherry

2 teaspoons chili paste

1 tablespoon cornstarch

½ teaspoon sugar

¼ teaspoon Szechuan peppercorns, lightly cracked if desired

Boil, stirring, until thickened, about 1 minute. Stir in:

One 10½-ounce package extra-firm tofu, pressed if desired, 80, and cubed

Heat through for 2 to 3 minutes. Arrange on a serving platter:

One 12-ounce package Chinese-style egg noodles, cooked

Spoon the tofu mixture over the noodles and garnish with:

¼ cup shredded peeled carrots

2 tablespoons sliced scallions

SZECHUAN PEPPERCORNS

The dried reddish-brown berries known as Szechuan peppercorns are not related to black peppercorns or chili peppers. The spice has a clean, spicy-woodsy fragrance that has made it popular in all regions of China for centuries. Szechuan peppercorns are sold in plastic packages. They keep well in a covered jar.

Toast Szechuan peppercorns in a dry skillet over medium heat until they begin to smoke (do not worry if a few blacken slightly) and then grind them in a mortar or spice grinder. Store excess powder in a jar. "Seasoned oil"—made by heating Szechuan peppercorns in peanut oil until they blacken, then straining the oil and discarding the peppercorns—makes a wonderful cooking oil for stir-fried dishes, or it may be used for dressing Chinese salads.

Smoked Tofu Burgers

6 servings

Tofu burgers are great for lunch or dinner. This flavorful patty mixture can also be baked as a loaf in a small loaf pan at 350°F for 40 to 45 minutes.

Soak in warm water to cover until softened, about 20 minutes:

½ ounce dried shiitake mushrooms

Drain, discarding the liquid, and squeeze out the excess water from the mushrooms. Chop the mushrooms, discarding the tough centers and stems. Heat in a large skillet over medium heat:

2 to 3 teaspoons chili sesame oil

Add the shiitakes along with:

1 cup finely chopped broccoli florets and stems

⅓ cup finely chopped red bell peppers

¼ cup sliced scallions

2 teaspoons finely chopped peeled fresh ginger

1½ teaspoons minced garlic

Cook, stirring, until tender, 4 to 5 minutes. Combine with:

One 6-ounce package smoked tofu, finely chopped

1 cup cooked brown rice

⅔ cup dry unseasoned breadcrumbs

2 large eggs, lightly beaten

1 tablespoon light or dark soy sauce

Remove to a food processor and pulse several times, until a spoonful of the mixture can be pressed into a ball. Shape the mixture into 6 patties (or burgers), using about ½ cup for each. Cook in a lightly greased skillet over medium heat until browned, 3 to 5 minutes each side. Serve hot on rolls.

Moo Shu Tempeh

12 pancakes; 6 servings

If cooking time does not allow this pancake preparation, warm flour tortillas will substitute nicely.

Stir together until crumbly:

⅓ cup boiling water
1 cup all-purpose flour

Shape into a ball and knead on a lightly floured surface until the dough is very smooth, about 10 minutes. Let stand, covered, for 30 minutes. Divide the dough into 12 equal pieces. Roll each piece into a ball, then into a 3-inch disk. Brush the top of 1 disk lightly with:

Sesame or vegetable oil

Top with a second disk. Roll out both disks together into a 6-inch pancake, being careful not to wrinkle the dough when rolling. Cook the pancakes in a lightly greased small skillet over medium to medium-high heat until the surface blisters and turns the color of parchment; turn often with chopsticks or tongs. Remove from the skillet and immediately separate the pancakes, using a sharp knife. Repeat with the remaining disks. Keep the pancakes warm, loosely covered, in a 200°F oven. At this point, the pancakes can be wrapped well and stored in the refrigerator or freezer. To reheat, arrange the pancakes slightly overlapping on a baking sheet and bake, covered, at 300°F until warm, 10 to 15 minutes.

Combine and let stand until the mushrooms are softened, 15 to 20 minutes:

1½ cups hot water
1 ounce dried shiitake mushrooms
¼ ounce dried wood or cloud ear mushrooms

Drain, reserving the liquid, and squeeze out the excess water from the mushrooms. Slice the mushrooms, discarding the tough centers and stems. Combine:

One 8-ounce package tempeh, cut into thin strips
1 tablespoon light or dark soy sauce

Heat in a wok or large skillet over medium heat:

1 teaspoon toasted sesame oil

Add:

3 large eggs, lightly beaten

Cook, without stirring, until set but still moist. Remove the egg pancake and cut into small pieces. Heat in the wok:

1 tablespoon toasted sesame oil

Add the tempeh mixture and stir-fry until lightly browned. Add the mushrooms along with:

One 8-ounce can bamboo shoots, drained and sliced
¼ cup sliced scallions
2 teaspoons minced peeled fresh ginger

Stir-fry for 2 to 3 minutes. Strain the mushroom soaking liquid through a fine-mesh sieve lined with dampened paper towels, measure it, and add water as needed to make ¾ cup. Combine with:

3 tablespoons light or dark soy sauce
3 tablespoons dry sherry
1 tablespoon cornstarch
1 teaspoon sugar

Pour into the wok and boil, stirring, until thickened, about 1 minute. Gently stir in the egg pieces. Spread each pancake with:

2 to 3 teaspoons plum sauce

Top each with about ⅓ cup of the tempeh mixture and then with:

1 scallion

Roll up, folding in the bottom end for eating.

Szechuan-Style "Hacked" Tempeh

4 servings

Tempeh is made by inoculating cooked skinless split soybeans with Rhizopus oligosporus *bacteria, shaping the beans into cakes, and allowing them to ferment for about 24 hours. The resulting supple slabs are sealed and refrigerated, ready for sale. Tempeh replaces the chicken in this traditional dish. Served chilled, the ingredients are tossed with a peanut sauce.*

Combine and let stand for 15 to 30 minutes:

One 8-ounce package tempeh, cut into ½-inch cubes

2 tablespoons light or dark soy sauce

2 to 3 teaspoons minced peeled fresh ginger

1 teaspoon minced garlic

½ teaspoon Szechuan peppercorns, cracked

Heat in a wok or medium skillet over medium heat:

1 tablespoon vegetable oil

Add the tempeh mixture and cook, stirring, until browned. Let cool, then refrigerate until chilled.

Combine and arrange on a serving platter:

2 cups sliced seeded peeled cucumbers

½ cup chopped red bell peppers

¼ cup sliced scallions

Spoon the tempeh mixture over the vegetables. Stir together until smooth and drizzle over the tempeh mixture:

¼ cup smooth peanut butter

2 tablespoons light or dark soy sauce

2 tablespoons rice vinegar

1 tablespoon dry sherry

3 to 4 teaspoons toasted sesame oil

1 teaspoon chili paste

Garnish with:

½ cup chopped red bell peppers

¼ cup sliced scallions

¼ cup chopped salted peanuts

Toss just before serving. If desired, serve with:

Chilled cooked rice noodles

ABOUT
PASTAS
& GRAINS

They say love comes when you least expect it, and that's what's been happening with grains. People pampered their whole lives with thick steaks, flashy salads, and rich desserts are suddenly finding that what they really crave are homely little wheat berries and bowls of creamy risotto.

Nowhere is our tendency to mix and match world flavors more evident than in our passion for pasta and noodles, which make up one of the largest and richest chapters in American cooking. Certainly Italy has made the greatest contribution. Italy's influence on our love affair with noodles is so great that the Italian word pasta *has become a part of our everyday language. In this chapter, we use* pasta *to refer to noodles of Italian origin and* noodles *when referring to eastern European and Asian dishes.*

Fresh Corn Risotto with Basil, Tomato, and Lime, 106

Pasta, Grains, and Nutrition

Pasta is made from wheat. From a nutritional standpoint, it joins other grain foods as the foundation of healthful diets and is the basis of many traditional cuisines. Many people believe that pasta is fattening and try to avoid eating it. This is a misunderstanding, as pasta is composed mainly of starch and protein, both relatively low in calories compared to fat. Most pasta dishes contain sauce, cheese, or vegetables that balance the starch and prevent unusual fluctuation in blood sugar levels. People who are concerned about calories should keep the portion sizes within reasonable limits, use tomato rather than cream sauces, and add just small amounts of cheese.

Dried pasta and fresh pasta are not better or worse, only different. That venerable favorite, spaghetti, is always a dried pasta made of the strongest durum wheat and water, never egg. On the other hand, fettuccine are flour and egg noodles that are best when fresh. However, in every case, a box of good-quality dried pasta is far better than any mediocre fresh pasta.

The quest for low-fat, high-fiber fare led to a much closer look at grains, which provide complex carbohydrates, protein, a very small amount of fat, many of the B-complex vitamins, and an essential array of minerals. By eating the six to eleven daily servings of grains recommended in federal dietary guidelines, you can consume the recommended amount of protein found in one to three small portions of meat, without the saturated fat and with much more fiber. The nutrition is more reliable if the grains are whole, varied, and supplemented by beans and some dairy products.

All true grains are fruits of grasses, and thus whole kernels are sometimes called berries. They are composed of three basic parts: the nutrient-dense germ, or seed, which contains protein and some oil; the endosperm, comprising carbohydrates and protein; and the bran, or high-fiber outer layer. Rice, barley, and oats also have an inedible outer husk; wheat, rye, and corn do not. If you eat all parts of the grain, other than the husk, you get all the vitamins, minerals, and other nutrients it contains—all the nourishment the seed needs to become a plant. It is common practice, however, to remove the bran and the germ and consume only the endosperm. White rice, for example, is endosperm only. So is the part of the wheat that is ground into white flour. Both these products are enriched with B vitamins and iron to replace, and even increase, the amounts lost when the bran and germ are discarded, but some things, including the vitamin E and fiber of the original, are left out.

Grains are much more alike than not, both in the cooking and the nutrition. Good health food stores and some supermarkets will stock more than a dozen distinct grains, including buckwheat and quinoa, which are not true grains, botanically speaking, but are similar enough to be treated as such.

Cooking Pasta

Fresh or dried, pasta should always be cooked in a large quantity of fiercely boiling salted water. Use about 1 tablespoon salt per 3 quarts water. Estimate 6 quarts water per 1 pound pasta, except for delicate filled pastas and very large noodles such as lasagne, which will need 9 to 12 quarts water. In either case, cooking more than 2 pounds of pasta at once invites problems of uneven cooking and draining. Adequate water and frequent stirring are the two keys to eliminating the problem of pasta sticking together. Adding oil to the water has little effect except to keep the pot from boiling over. Unless the strands are outrageously long and cannot fit into the pot without cracking, do not break pasta before cooking.

Since pasta cooks quickly and is at its best as soon as it is cooked, have everything ready before you start—the sauce prepared, a large colander set in the sink for draining, and a serving bowl and dishes warming in the oven. Once the salted water is rapidly boiling, add the pasta all at once. As soon as the pasta softens slightly, give it a stir, partially cover the pot, and let it continue to boil vigorously, stirring often to keep it from sticking together.

Different pastas have different cooking times, and the only test for doneness is to lift a piece from the pot and taste it. Italians consider the ideal state *al dente* (to the tooth), which means tender but firm—no raw flour taste and enough firmness to give a pleasing resistance to the bite. Start testing fresh pasta and very thin shapes after about 30 seconds, spaghetti and linguine after 4 minutes, and thick macaroni after 8 minutes. Once the pasta tastes done, do not waste a moment—empty the pot immediately into the colander and quickly toss the colander to rid the pasta of as much water as possible.

Combine the drained pasta with its sauce over heat if possible for maximum flavor, or simply toss the hot pasta and sauce in a warmed serving bowl. Either way, pasta is best eaten hot without delay.

Rinse pasta only if destined to be baked or to be eaten cool in a salad.

Cooking Grains

Grains can be simmered on the stovetop, in the oven, or in the microwave (which won't save time but will yield predictably good texture, with no pot to wash). The pressure cooker can be a big time-saver with long-cooking wheat berries and hulled barley, but it is important to consult your owner's manual for instructions; some recommend against cooking any grains, and others require that the grain be cooked in an aluminum-foil-covered bowl to prevent the possibility that loose bits of hull or starch will clog the steam vent.

Wheat berries and other large whole grains are commonly presoaked for 8 hours or overnight to hasten their cooking time. A soaking shortcut is to heat the grain and liquid to a full boil on top of the stove and simmer for 2 minutes; remove from the heat and let stand, covered, for 1 hour, until some kernels begin to split. Or microwave the grain and liquid in a covered casserole on high for 10 minutes and then on medium for 5 minutes; let stand, covered, for 1 hour. Either way, cooking the grain in the soaking water retains nutrients. Note that presoaking is not always called for when the grain is to be used in a salad, because a firmer texture is desired.

Be generous with the size and the width of the pot when cooking grains, as they will cook fluffier if not clumped together. With more than 1 cup of grains, you will get fluffier results if you use a wide saucepan, a Dutch oven, or even a deep skillet with a tight lid. Fine-textured and small grains, such as cornmeal and amaranth, tend to stick to the pot and scorch if not stirred often, especially if cooked without fat. Using a double boiler or the microwave reduces the risk, as well as the need to stir as much, by removing the grain from direct heat. Oven baking yields consistently dry, fluffy results with rice and barley if the casserole is wide and heavy enough, because the heat comes from all sides and not just the bottom of the pot.

Buying and Storing Grains

An important general consideration is freshness. Any whole grain, for example, whether brown rice or millet, is much more perishable than a refined product such as white rice or pearl barley. While pearl barley will keep for at least 6 months in an airtight container in a cool pantry, millet should be refrigerated to be sure of preventing rancidity. So it is wise to buy these in a store that does a heavy volume of business in whole grains and perhaps even keeps them in a specially cooled section. Products high in oil content, especially quinoa and wheat germ, turn rancid fast and should be refrigerated once you get them home or break the vacuum seal of the jar. Buy other whole grains in amounts you can use within 1 month and store them in tightly covered jars in the pantry or refrigerate or freeze them in freezer bags or sealed containers for up to 2 months. Signs of rancidity are an off odor before cooking and a bitter taste when cooked. Grains purchased loose usually need to be rinsed and picked over for bits of chaff or debris. Place the grain in a large fine-mesh sieve set in a pot large enough to hold it; rinse under cold water, raking the grain with your fingers. Let debris rise to the surface and remove it. Drain well. Grains sold in boxes are generally clean and ready for the pot.

Cooked grains can be refrigerated for at least 3 days—and a few days longer if cooked with water and not stock or other perishable ingredients. They reheat beautifully in the microwave. Spread portions on individual plates, cover with plastic wrap, and microwave on high for 1 to 2 minutes per serving. To reheat a bowlful, sprinkle the surface lightly with water, cover with plastic wrap or a lid, and microwave on high for about 1½ minutes per cup; stir before serving. To reheat on the stovetop, put a thin layer of water in a saucepan, add the grain, and simmer, covered, over medium heat until hot.

TOASTING GRAINS

Toasting a grain before you simmer it in liquid brings out the fragrance. You can spread it in a heavy saucepan or skillet and heat over medium heat, stirring often, until the grain smells rich and toasted, usually just a few minutes; be careful not to scorch the smallest grains, such as amaranth and millet. Heating or melting some oil or butter in the pan before you stir in and toast the grain will add flavor and help keep the kernels separate, for fluffier texture, when they cook; this preparation is called a pilaf and often includes vegetables lightly browned with the grain.

To toast grains in the oven, spread them on a baking sheet and bake in a preheated 350°F oven for about 10 minutes, stirring once only.

Spaghetti with Eggplant

4 to 8 servings

The sauce for this Sicilian dish can be made several hours ahead if desired. The night or morning before cooking, spread on a baking sheet lined with a double layer of paper towels:

1 medium eggplant, unpeeled, cut into ½-inch cubes

Sprinkle generously with:

Salt

Cover with another double layer of paper towels. Set a cutting board or another baking sheet on top and weight with heavy cans. Let the eggplant drain for at least 8 hours. Heat in a large skillet over medium heat:

3 tablespoons extra-virgin olive oil

Add the eggplant and cook, stirring, until tender and golden. Add and cook for about 15 seconds:

2 large cloves garlic, minced

Add:

7 medium, ripe tomatoes, peeled, seeded, and chopped

2 medium bell peppers, preferably yellow, roasted, peeled, and seeded, 58, and finely chopped

Cook, stirring frequently, until the sauce is thickened, about 10 minutes. Stir in:

½ cup fresh basil leaves, coarsely chopped

1 tablespoon drained capers

2 large green olives, preferably Sicilian, pitted and chopped

Salt and ground black pepper to taste

Meanwhile, bring to a rolling boil in a large pot:

6 quarts water

2 tablespoons salt

Add and cook until tender but firm:

1 pound spaghetti

Drain the pasta and toss with the sauce. Cheese is not traditionally served with this dish.

Tagliatelle with Wilted Greens

4 to 8 servings

Make this dish as spicy as you like by using more or fewer chili peppers. Remember, much of a chili's heat is in the seeds, so that removing them will temper the dish.

Bring to a rolling boil in a large pot:

6 quarts water

2 tablespoons salt

Add and cook until tender but firm:

1¼ pounds fresh tagliatelle, or 1 pound dried

Meanwhile, heat in a large skillet or wok over medium heat:

2 to 4 tablespoons olive oil

Add and cook until barely colored:

¼ cup minced onion

4 cloves garlic, chopped

1 to 3 fresh hot chili peppers, seeded and finely diced

Increase the heat to high and drop in:

3 big handfuls fresh arugula or mixed tart salad greens

Cook, stirring, until the greens are wilted. Drain the pasta and toss it with the greens, adding:

Salt and ground black pepper to taste

Shavings of pecorino cheese or crumbled fresh goat cheese

Serve immediately.

Egg Noodles with Brown Butter and Nuts

Place in a small pan:

8 tablespoons (1 stick) unsalted butter

Gradually brown the butter over medium heat until golden brown and a nutty aroma arises. Add, if desired, any one or all of the following:

¼ cup chopped nuts, such as cashews, roasted peanuts, pecans, toasted almonds, pine nuts, or toasted walnuts

1 teaspoon minced garlic (optional)

1 tablespoon chopped fresh herbs, or 1 teaspoon dried, such as thyme, basil, chives, parsley, oregano, and/or tarragon (optional)

Grated zest of small lemon (optional)

Toss with:

1 pound dried egg noodles, cooked until tender but firm

Use your imagination and see what is in your refrigerator and spice drawer.

Summer Squash and Pasta

4 to 6 servings

Steam until tender:

1 pound summer squash, cut into ½-inch-thick batons or dice

Toss in a bowl with:

1 pound mostaccioli, penne, or macaroni, cooked and drained

½ to ¾ cup *Pesto Sauce*, right

Pesto Sauce

Enough for 1 pound pasta

This classic sauce from Genoa needs to be made with fresh basil. Pesto is traditionally tossed with trenette, a flat ribbon pasta similar to linguine but fresh. If freezing, add the nuts and cheese after thawing.

Process to a rough paste in a food processor:

2 cups loosely packed fresh basil leaves

⅓ cup pine nuts

2 medium cloves garlic, peeled

½ cup grated Parmesan cheese

With the machine running, slowly pour through the feed tube:

½ cup extra-virgin olive oil

If the sauce seems dry (it should be a thick paste), add a little more olive oil. Season with:

Salt and ground black pepper to taste

Use immediately or store in a covered glass jar in the refrigerator for up to 1 week.

Eggplant Lasagne Bundles

4 to 8 servings

Peel, if desired, and cut into ½-inch-thick rounds:

2 pounds eggplant

Steam the eggplant in batches over boiling salted water until very soft but still intact, 10 to 15 minutes. Spread the cooked slices on a platter and sprinkle with:

½ teaspoon sea salt

For the béchamel, melt in a saucepan over medium-low heat:

6 tablespoons (¾ stick) unsalted butter

With a wooden spoon, stir in:

6 tablespoons all-purpose flour

Cook, stirring, until the mixture has bubbled and cooked for 2 minutes to remove the raw taste of the flour. Do not allow the flour to darken. Off the heat, gradually whisk in:

3 cups milk

When the milk is completely incorporated, continue to whisk until smooth and lump free. Cook, stirring, over low heat until the béchamel has thickened to the consistency of thick cream. If you notice any lumps in the sauce, strain the béchamel through a fine-mesh sieve and transfer to a clean pan. Add:

¼ cup tomato paste
½ teaspoon sea salt

Whisk until smooth. Set aside, whisking every 5 minutes to prevent a skin from forming. Preheat the oven to 375°F. Smear a 12 x 9-inch lasagne pan with:

2 tablespoons unsalted butter

Bring to a boil in a large pot:

6 quarts water

Generously salt the water and add in 2 or 3 batches:

8 fresh lasagne noodles or equivalent of good-quality imported dried noodles

The fresh pasta will cook in 30 seconds after the water has resumed boiling. Scoop the noodles from the pot with a strainer and let drain in a colander. Lay them out on a clean work surface. Spread each noodle with 1 to 2 tablespoons of the béchamel. On the bottom half of each noodle, lay out the cooked egg-plant slices, then cover them with:

12 ounces fresh mozzarella, thinly sliced
⅔ cup grated Parmesan cheese

Fold the top half of the pasta over the eggplant and cheese, spread the surface of each bundle with an additional 1 tablespoon béchamel, if desired, then fold each side in toward the middle. You now have a rectangular pasta bundle. Spread half of the remaining béchamel sauce over the bottom of the buttered pan. Top with the pasta bundles, seam-side down, overlapping them a bit if necessary. Top with the remaining béchamel and sprinkle over the surface:

⅓ cup grated Parmesan cheese

Dot with:

2 tablespoons unsalted butter, cut into bits

Bake for 15 minutes. Increase the oven temperature to 400°F and bake until a golden crust forms on top, about 5 minutes more. Remove from the oven and let rest for 5 to 10 minutes before serving.

Roasted Vegetable Lasagne

8 to 10 servings

The vegetables in this lasagne are first roasted, giving them extra flavor and character. They can be prepared a day ahead and stored in the refrigerator. This version is made without the traditional tomato sauce, incorporating fresh tomatoes into the layers instead. The zucchini and eggplant are roasted together, divided between two pans, while the tomatoes are roasted in their own pan because they release a lot of juice, which would inhibit browning of the zucchini and eggplant. If your oven will hold two pans side by side, then you will be able to roast everything at the same time on two racks. If not, roast the tomatoes as a separate batch. The lasagne is covered during a portion of the baking time because there is no tomato sauce; use a layer of breadcrumbs if desired.

Position a rack in the lower third of the oven and another in the upper third. Preheat the oven to 450°F. Lightly oil a 13 x 9 x 3-inch baking or lasagne pan.

Place in a large bowl:

2 medium-large eggplants (about 3 pounds), quartered and cut into ½-inch-thick slices

6 medium zucchini (about 3 pounds), cut into ½-inch-thick slices

Pour over the vegetables:

½ cup olive oil, preferably extra virgin

1 teaspoon salt

½ teaspoon ground black pepper

Toss well to coat all the vegetable pieces with oil and remove to 2 roasting pans. Position the pans side by side in the oven or place 1 on each rack if they do not fit side by side. Roast for 20 minutes. Toss the vegetables with a metal spatula, scraping up the browned bits. Continue to roast until well browned and soft, about 20 minutes more. Remove to a large bowl. Place in a roasting pan:

3 pounds ripe tomatoes, halved crosswise

Drizzle over the tomatoes:

2 tablespoons olive oil, preferably extra virgin

Generous amount of salt

Ground black pepper to taste

Roast the tomatoes until soft and slightly golden, about 45 minutes. Remove the tomatoes with their juice and all the oil to the bowl with the vegetables and stir together well. Reduce the oven temperature to 375°F.

Bring to a rolling boil in a large pot:

8 quarts water

2 tablespoons salt

Meanwhile, stir together well in a medium bowl:

1 pound ricotta cheese

2 large eggs

½ cup grated Parmesan cheese

½ teaspoon salt, or to taste

Ground black pepper to taste

Ground nutmeg to taste (optional)

Have ready:

1 pound mozzarella cheese (preferably fresh), shredded

When the water boils, add and cook until barely tender:

1 pound fresh, or 1 pound dried lasagne

Drain and separate the noodles. Keep in a bowl of ice water. To assemble the lasagne, arrange a layer of noodles over the bottom of the prepared pan. Spread with one-third of the ricotta mixture. Sprinkle one-quarter of the mozzarella over the ricotta mixture along with:

2 tablespoons Parmesan cheese

Ground black pepper to taste

Spoon one-third of the roasted vegetables on top. Add another layer of noodles and continue layering the lasagne until all the ingredients are used. You will have 4 layers of pasta and 3 layers of filling. Sprinkle the final one-quarter of the mozzarella over the top along with:

2 tablespoons Parmesan cheese

1 cup fresh breadcrumbs (optional)

Cover the pan with aluminum foil and bake for 30 minutes. Uncover and continue to bake until golden and bubbly, about 15 minutes more. Let stand for 15 minutes before serving.

EGGPLANT

The peak season for eggplants is midsummer to midautumn. Select eggplants of whatever sort that are heavy for their size, with taut skin, a fresh, green cap and stem, and not a single soft spot, cut, or bruise. In standard types, the skin should be glossy. As a rule, small to medium eggplants are the choicest, being the youngest. If the eggplant seems old and the flesh is dark, it may need salting to draw out its bitterness. Generously sprinkle pieces with coarse salt. Place them in a nonreactive colander and let drain for 30 to 60 minutes. Turn onto a thick towel and gently press out excess moisture. Lightly rub the pieces in the towel to rub off the salt and dry them.

ELECTRIC RICE COOKERS

Electric rice cookers are ingenious devices that make preparing white or brown rice a snap. Most rice cookers have a large cooking chamber (often lined with a non-stick coating) that rests above an electric heating element. Most also come with a perforated insert that fits near the bottom of the cooking pot, transforming the rice cooker into a steamer for vegetables, fish, and other foods. Follow the manufacturer's instructions, but keep in mind that some rice cookers imported from Asia come with directions that assume the rice has been rinsed or soaked. When cooking dry—not rinsed or soaked—rice in a rice cooker, use ¼ to ½ cup less water per cup than you would in stove-top cooking.

Basic Cooked White Rice

3 cups; 4 servings

A cook needs to know two things about rice. The first is whether or not the bran and germ are still attached. If so, it is brown rice, making it more nutritious, more perishable, and slower cooking than white rice. The second thing is the length of the grain. The longer the grain, the less starchy and plump the rice. Use 2 cups water for soft, tender rice or 1 ¾ to 1 ⅞ cups for firmer grains. Use ¼ cup less, either way, when cooking medium-grain white rice. Do not stir, except as directed, as the rice will turn gummy.

I. Bring to a boil in a medium saucepan:

1¾ to 2 cups water

1 tablespoon butter or vegetable oil (optional)

¼ to ½ teaspoon salt

Add and stir once:

1 cup long-grain white rice

Cover and cook over very low heat until all the water is absorbed, 15 to 18 minutes. Do not lift the cover before the end of cooking. Let stand, covered, for 5 to 10 minutes before serving.

II. This method is popular in the American South, Latin America, and parts of Europe.

Spread in a large, broad, shallow, heavy saucepan to a depth of only 2 or 3 grains:

1 cup long-grain or medium-grain white rice

Add just enough liquid to cover the rice by ½ inch or the thickness of your hand. Bring to a gentle boil and stir once. Cook, uncovered, over low heat until the liquid is almost absorbed, about 5 minutes. Cover the saucepan and continue to cook for 15 to 18 minutes. Do not lift the cover before the end of cooking. Let stand, covered, for 5 to 10 minutes before serving.

Fried Rice

4 servings

Fried rice is popular as much for its taste as for its rapid preparation and versatility. Remember to always begin with cold cooked rice (a mixture of part white and part brown is excellent). The variations are endless. Add small amounts (about ½ cup) of cooked cut-up broccoli, carrots, green beans, squash, or sweet potatoes or thawed frozen green peas. For additional flavor, sprinkle with toasted sesame seeds or chopped peanuts. Drizzle with a little toasted sesame oil or soy sauce at the table.

Whisk together:

4 eggs

½ teaspoon salt

Heat a large nonstick skillet or wok over medium heat until hot enough to evaporate a drop of water on contact. Pour in and tilt the skillet to coat:

1 tablespoon vegetable oil

Heat until very hot. Add the eggs all at once and as they bubble up around the edges, push them to the center, tilting the skillet to cook the eggs evenly. Break the cooked eggs into clumps. When the eggs are set, remove to a bowl. Pour into the hot skillet and heat until hot:

2 tablespoons vegetable oil

Add and cook, stirring to coat the grains with oil, for 3 minutes:

3 to 4 cups cold cooked rice (1 to 1⅓ cups uncooked)

1 teaspoon minced peeled fresh ginger

Stir in the cooked eggs along with:

½ cup thin diagonal scallion slices

Serve immediately.

Thai Coconut Rice

4 to 6 servings

Thai, or jasmine, rice is a long-grain rice with a soft, slightly sticky consistency. If using domestically grown jasmine rice, there is no need to rinse it. Imported jasmine rice should probably be rinsed. Canned unsweetened coconut milk is available in many supermarkets or wherever Asian groceries are sold.

Bring to a boil in a large saucepan:

1 cup canned unsweetened coconut milk and 1 cup water

1 cup jasmine rice

1 thin slice peeled fresh ginger

¾ teaspoon salt

Stir once, cover, and cook over very low heat until the liquid is absorbed and the rice is tender, about 20 minutes. Meanwhile lightly toast, stirring, in a small skillet over medium-low heat:

⅓ cup flaked or shredded unsweetened dried coconut

Sprinkle over the cooked rice along with:

Fresh cilantro leaves (optional)

Persian Rice

4 to 6 servings

Prepare in a nonstick skillet so the rice can be easily inverted, showing off its deliciously crisp crust.

Preheat the oven to 350°F.

Bring to a boil in a large pot:

16 cups (4 quarts) water

1 tablespoon salt

Stir in:

2 cups white basmati rice

One 1-inch cinnamon stick

3 whole cloves

3 black peppercorns

¼ teaspoon cardamom seeds

Cook, uncovered, stirring occasionally, until the rice is almost tender, about 10 minutes. Drain and let stand in a sieve until ready to use.

(Leave the spices in the rice.) Melt in a large ovenproof nonstick skillet over medium heat:

8 tablespoons (1 stick) butter

Spoon off 3 tablespoons and reserve. Add to the remaining butter in the skillet:

1 cup thinly sliced onions

¼ teaspoon saffron threads

Cook, stirring, over medium heat until the onions are golden, about 8 minutes. Spread the onions in an even layer in the skillet. Stir into the cooked rice:

2 tablespoons diced dried apricots

2 tablespoons dried sweet or sour cherries or golden raisins

Spoon the rice over the onions; smooth the top of the rice with the back of a large spoon and press down very firmly to pack it. Drizzle the reserved butter evenly over the top. Cover with a double layer of aluminum foil, crimping the edges and pressing down on the top. Bake for 1 hour. Let stand, covered, for 10 minutes. Uncover and invert a large round platter over the skillet. Protecting your hands with a dish towel, turn the skillet and platter over, allowing the rice to drop onto the platter. Sprinkle with:

¼ cup chopped shelled pistachios

Basic Pilaf

4 servings

Rice stirred in hot butter or oil before simmering is very flavorful and fluffy, especially if you use basmati rice. The preparation is known as a pilaf, and it traditionally calls for seasonings to be sautéed in the pot with the rice. The name can be traced to the Persian pilau. All kinds of variations are found in the Middle East, the Caucasus, and India.

Melt in a large saucepan or deep skillet over low heat:

2 tablespoons butter

Add and cook, stirring, until golden, about 8 minutes:

½ cup chopped onions

Add and cook, stirring, until coated, about 3 minutes:

1 cup white basmati rice

Stir in:

2 cups water or *Vegetable Stock,*17
½ teaspoon salt (if using water)

Bring to a boil. Stir once, cover, and cook over low heat until the liquid is absorbed and the rice is tender, about 15 minutes. Do not stir. Let stand, covered, for 5 minutes before serving. Sprinkle with:

2 tablespoons chopped walnuts, toasted, or 2 tablespoons chopped fresh parsley

Two-Grain Date Pilaf

4 to 6 servings

Rice and bulgur spiced with a cinnamon stick and topped with a few chopped dates make this recipe an especially exotic pilaf.

Melt in a large saucepan or deep skillet over medium heat:

2 tablespoons butter

Add and cook, stirring, until golden, about 8 minutes:

½ cup chopped onions

Add:

1 cup white basmati rice
1 cup bulgur or cracked wheat
One 1-inch cinnamon stick

Stir to coat with the butter. Add:

4 cups water or *Vegetable Stock,*17
1 teaspoon salt (if using water)

Bring to a boil. Stir once, cover, and cook over medium-low heat until the liquid is absorbed and the rice is tender, about 20 minutes. Uncover and let stand for 5 minutes.

Meanwhile, melt in a small skillet over medium heat:

1 tablespoon butter

Add and cook, stirring, until heated through, about 1 minute:

¼ cup diced dates

Spoon the pilaf into a serving dish and top with the dates. Serve immediately.

Lentil and Rice Pilaf with Toasted Cumin Seeds

4 to 6 servings

Whole cumin seeds lend a wonderful aroma to this dish. Serve as a side dish or as a main course topped with cooked vegetables.

Stir into a medium saucepan of boiling water:

½ cup lentils, picked over and rinsed

Boil, uncovered, for 10 minutes; drain. Heat in a large saucepan or deep skillet over low heat:

2 tablespoons vegetable oil

Add and cook just until sizzling, about 1 minute:

1 clove garlic, finely chopped
½ teaspoon cumin seeds

Add the lentils along with:

1 cup white basmati rice

Stir to combine. Add:

2 cups *Vegetable Stock,*17

¼ to ½ teaspoon salt

Bring to a boil. Stir once, cover, and cook over medium-low heat until the stock is absorbed and the rice and lentils are tender, about 15 minutes. Uncover and let stand for 5 minutes. Meanwhile, toast in a small skillet over medium heat:

¼ cup chopped walnuts

Sprinkle over the pilaf and serve.

Wild Rice with Sautéed Mushrooms

4 to 6 servings

Use any combination of exotic and/or cultivated mushrooms in this simple dish. Combine in a large saucepan:

3 cups water

1 cup wild rice, rinsed and drained

1 teaspoon salt (optional)

Bring to a boil. Stir once, cover, and simmer over low heat until the water is absorbed and the rice is fluffy and tender, 35 to 55 minutes. About 10 minutes before the rice is done, heat in a large saucepan or deep skillet over medium-high heat:

¼ cup olive oil

Add and cook, stirring, until lightly browned, 5 to 8 minutes:

2 cups sliced button or cremini mushrooms

1 cup sliced shiitake or porcini mushroom caps

1 cup chopped onions

Add and cook, stirring, until combined, about 2 minutes:

¼ cup finely chopped fresh parsley

2 cloves garlic, finely chopped

1 teaspoon fresh thyme leaves, or ¼ teaspoon dried

Stir in the cooked wild rice along with:

Salt and ground black pepper to taste

Cover and cook over medium heat until heated through, about 5 minutes. If desired, sprinkle with:

¼ cup sliced unblanched almonds, toasted

Oven-Baked Brown Rice with Mushrooms

4 to 6 servings

Brown rice and mushrooms share the same deep, earthy flavor. Serve this simple preparation topped with broccoli or a mixture of cooked vegetables.

Preheat the oven to 350°F.

Melt or heat in a 2-quart stovetop-to-oven casserole over medium-high heat:

3 tablespoons butter or olive oil

Add and cook, stirring, until the mushrooms are lightly browned, about 8 minutes:

1½ cups coarsely chopped mushrooms

½ cup chopped onions
1 clove garlic, finely chopped

Add and stir until coated:

1 cup long-grain brown rice
⅛ teaspoon ground black pepper

Add:

2¼ cups *Vegetable Stock,*17
¼ teaspoon salt

Bring to a boil. Cover and bake until the rice is tender and the stock is absorbed, about 45 minutes. Let stand, covered, for 10 minutes before serving.

Barley and Mushroom "Risotto"

8 servings

This is not a real risotto because it does not contain rice, but it is made in the same way. To serve this dish as a main course for 4 people, omit the salt and stir in ½ to 1 cup grated Parmesan cheese just before serving.

Heat in a large, deep skillet over medium heat until the foam subsides:

4 to 6 tablespoons (½ to ¾ stick) butter

Add and cook, stirring, until tender but not brown, about 7 minutes:

1⅓ cups finely chopped onions

Stir in and cook until softened:

8 ounces shiitake mushrooms, stems removed and caps diced

Reduce the heat to medium-low. Add and stir until glazed with butter:

1 cup pearl barley

Add and cook, stirring, until the liquid is absorbed:

⅔ cup dry white wine
1 tablespoon mashed or finely minced garlic
½ teaspoon salt
½ teaspoon ground black pepper

Warm, but do not allow to simmer, in a saucepan set over very low heat:

6 cups *Vegetable Stock,*17

Keep the stock warm. Stir 2 cups of the vegetable stock into the barley. Simmer slowly, stirring occasionally, until the stock is almost absorbed. Add the remaining stock ½ cup at a time, allowing each addition to be absorbed before adding the next and stirring often. The barley needs 45 to 60 minutes' cooking to become tender. If you run low on stock while the barley is still very underdone, reduce the heat. If you do run out of stock, finish cooking with hot water.

Fresh Corn Risotto with Basil, Tomato, and Lime

4 to 6 servings

Make this delicate risotto at the height of the corn season. The lime juice adds a distinctive flavor when combined with the natural acidity of the tomato and the sweet, starchy taste of the corn and the rice.

Combine:

1 cup diced seeded peeled ripe tomatoes

2 tablespoons chopped fresh basil

1 tablespoon fresh lime juice

¼ teaspoon salt, or to taste

Bring to a simmer:

5 cups *Vegetable Stock, 17*

Cut:

2 cups corn kernels from 4 or 5 large ears

Puree 1 cup of the corn kernels in a food processor. Heat in a large saucepan or deep skillet over medium heat until the foam subsides:

2 tablespoons butter, preferably unsalted

Add and cook, stirring, until translucent, about 5 minutes:

½ cup finely chopped scallions (white part only)

Add:

1½ cups Italian rice or American medium-grain rice

Stir to coat with the butter. Add:

½ cup dry white wine

Cook, stirring, until absorbed. Add 1 cup of the simmering stock and cook, stirring, over medium-low heat until the stock is absorbed. Add the remaining stock, ½ cup at a time, cooking and stirring until the liquid is almost completely absorbed before adding more, about 15 minutes in all. Stir in the reserved pureed corn and another ½ cup stock; continue to cook, stirring and adding stock as needed, until the rice is tender but with a slight firmness to the center of the grain, 5 to 10 minutes more, or longer, depending on the rice. Stir in the corn kernels and the fresh tomato mixture. Season with:

Salt and ground black pepper to taste

Spoon into warmed soup bowls and sprinkle each serving with:

Grated Parmesan cheese

RULES FOR RISOTTO

- Use a large, heavy saucepan and never cover the cooking risotto. Anticipate about 20 minutes' cooking time.

- Use a medium-grain rice, never long-grain. First choices are Italian imports, always "superfino" grade—Arborio, Carnaroli, Vialone Nano, Roma, or Balso. Second choice is American medium-grain rice.

- Add small quantities of simmering stock to the risotto and stir almost constantly.

- At the end of cooking, the rice should be creamy in consistency and tender to the taste but still have a little "bite." Let the risotto stand off the heat for a few minutes before serving.

Leftover Risotto Pancake (Risotto al Salto)

4 servings

Place in a large bowl:

1 to 2 cups cold leftover risotto, above and opposite

Stir in, 1 tablespoon at a time:

1 large egg, lightly beaten

If the risotto is very soft, do not add all of the egg. Heat in a large nonstick skillet over medium-low heat until foamy:

2 tablespoons butter

Add the risotto mixture by tablespoonfuls for small pancakes or by ½- to 1-cup measures for larger pancakes. Cook, undisturbed, until the bottoms are browned and crisp, about 5 minutes.

Carefully turn and brown the second side, about 5 minutes. If making small pancakes, several can be fried at once, but fry larger pancakes 1 at a time. Before serving, sprinkle the pancakes with:

Grated Parmesan cheese

Risotto Primavera

8 first-course servings; 6 main-course servings

This makes a great first or main course.
Combine and let stand for
10 minutes:

**3 generous pinches of saffron
threads**

1 cup hot *Vegetable Stock,* 17

Melt in a large, heavy saucepan over
medium heat:

3 tablespoons butter

Stir in:

1 medium onion, minced

Cook over low heat until soft and
clear. Meanwhile, simmer over
medium heat:

9 cups *Vegetable Stock,* 17

Increase the heat under the onions
to medium and stir in:

**1 pound Italian rice or American
medium-grain rice**

Cook, stirring often, until the rice is
chalky in appearance, about 5 minutes. Add:

½ cup dry white wine

Stir until absorbed. Add the saffron
mixture and simmer, uncovered,
stirring often, until absorbed. Add
the vegetable stock, 1 cup at a time,
and simmer and stir continuously
until absorbed. (If desired, when
half of the stock has been used and
the rice is still quite firm, the risotto
can be removed from the heat and
refrigerated, covered, for up to
2 days. To finish the risotto, reheat

and continue.) Add the remaining
stock, 1 cup at a time, until the rice
is tender but still has some "bite."
It should be creamy and not stiff.
Fold in:

**1 to 1½ cups grated Parmesan
cheese**

**1½ cups sautéed spring vegetables,
cut into bite-sized pieces**

Season with:

**Salt and ground black pepper
to taste**

Let rest for a few minutes, then
serve in warmed soup dishes. If
desired, serve with:

Grated Parmesan cheese

Oven-Baked Polenta

6 servings

In this version of polenta, the pre-liminary cooking can be cut in half because the polenta finishes cooking as it bakes in the oven.

Melt or heat in a large saucepan over medium heat:

2 tablespoons butter or olive oil

Add and cook, stirring, until translucent, about 5 minutes:

½ cup finely chopped onions

Stir in and bring to a boil:

3 cups water, or 1½ cups *Vegetable Stock*, 17, and 1½ cups water

Stir together:

2 cups water, or 1 cup *Vegetable Stock*, 17, and 1 cup water

1½ cups yellow cornmeal

Gradually stir into the boiling liquid; cook, stirring constantly, over low heat until the cornmeal is thickened, about 15 minutes.

Preheat the oven to 350°F. Lightly butter a shallow 2-quart baking dish. Pour half of the polenta into the baking dish. Smooth with a spatula. Have ready:

4 ounces Gruyère cheese, thinly slivered

4 ounces mozzarella cheese, thinly slivered

½ cup grated Parmesan cheese

Top the layer of polenta with half of the cheese. Spread the remaining polenta on top and sprinkle with the remaining cheese. Pour over:

½ cup heavy cream, half-and-half, or milk

Bake until the top is browned and bubbly, 35 to 45 minutes. Let stand for 10 minutes before serving.

Posole

4 servings

Posole is a hearty Latin American stew served on feast days and other special occasions. This is one of many variations on a piquant Southwest classic. The day before cooking the posole, start the chili paste.

Place in a bowl and cover with boiling water by 1 inch.

6 to 8 dried New Mexico (red Anaheim) peppers, seeded

6 to 8 dried chili negro (also called chilaca) peppers, seeded

Soak for at least 8 hours or overnight. Drain and finely chop in a food processor, then press through a food mill or sieve. Refrigerate until ready to use.

For the posole, heat in a large saucepan over medium heat:

1 tablespoon olive oil

Add and cook, stirring, until translucent, about 5 minutes:

1 cup chopped onions

Add and cook, stirring, until the bell peppers are softened, about 3 minutes:

½ cup chopped red bell peppers

1 tablespoon chopped garlic

½ teaspoon dried oregano

Stir in:

2 cups drained canned hominy or thawed frozen hominy

2 cups *Vegetable Stock*, 17

Bring to a boil. Stir in ¼ to ⅓ cup (to taste) of the chili paste along with:

¼ cup chopped seeded fresh Anaheim peppers or canned green chili peppers

1 tablespoon chopped seeded fresh jalapeño peppers

Simmer, partially covered, over low heat for 30 minutes. Just before serving, stir in:

⅓ cup fresh orange juice

2 tablespoons fresh lemon juice

1 teaspoon salt, or to taste

Serve over rice.

HOMINY

Dried corn that has been treated with an alkali to remove its hulls is called hominy or slaked corn. The process makes the niacin in corn available as a nutrient and thus prevents pellagra. The Native Americans who first made hominy used wood ash or lime; today slaked lime or lye is most common. Cracked into a coarse meal, hominy becomes hominy grits; ground into flour, it is masa harina, used to make tortillas. Whole dried hominy made from white corn is also known as posole; cooked, it is available canned and, in some places, frozen. Hominy is sometimes available as golden (made from yellow corn) and white. Dried hominy needs to be soaked overnight, drained, and simmered until tender before use. Canned hominy needs only to be rinsed before use.

Quinoa-Stuffed Acorn Squash

4 servings

Quinoa, pronounced "keenwa," was cultivated in the Andes by Inca farmers. Botanically, it is not a true grain, but a relative of spinach and beets. Quinoa can be substituted for bulgur or white rice in pilafs and salads.

Preheat the oven to 350°F. Arrange cut side down in a baking pan:

3 acorn squash, halved and seeded

Add ½ inch water to the pan and cover with aluminum foil. Bake until the squash are tender, 45 to 55 minutes. Leave the oven on. Let the squash cool. Heat in a large skillet over medium heat:

1 tablespoon butter

Add and cook, stirring, until golden, about 8 minutes:

½ cup chopped onions

Stir in:

½ cup quinoa, rinsed and drained

Heat, stirring, until toasted, about 3 minutes. Stir in:

1 cup *Vegetable Stock*, 17

Bring to a boil, reduce the heat, and simmer, covered, for 15 minutes. Uncover and let cool slightly. Scoop out and dice the pulp of 2 squash halves. Turn the other 4 halves cut side up and season with:

½ teaspoon salt

⅛ teaspoon ground black pepper

Combine the quinoa and diced squash. Stir in:

¼ cup chopped hazelnuts or whole unblanched almonds, toasted

2 tablespoons chopped fresh parsley

2 tablespoons grated Parmesan cheese

Spoon into the 4 squash cavities, distributing evenly. Sprinkle the tops with:

2 tablespoons grated Parmesan cheese

Bake until heated through, about 20 minutes.

Whole-Grain Berries with Sautéed Onions and Dried Fruits

4 servings

Fully cooked whole-grain berries make an excellent dish when tossed with golden sautéed onions and plumped diced dried fruits. Add a cinnamon stick to the mixture for the final heating—its aroma will permeate the grains.

Soak in water to cover by 2 inches:

1 cup wheat, spelt, or kamut berries, or a combination

Let stand overnight. Drain if needed and add to:

8 cups boiling salted water

Gently simmer, uncovered, until tender but still chewy, 45 to 60 minutes. Drain.

Melt or heat in a large skillet over medium heat:

2 tablespoons butter or olive oil

Add and cook, stirring, until golden, 8 to 10 minutes:

1 cup chopped onions

Add:

1 cup diced mixed dried fruits, such as dried apricots, pitted prunes, golden or dark raisins, dried currants, dried cherries, and/or dried cranberries

Stir to blend.

Stir in:

Cooked wheat, spelt, or kamut berries

One 2-inch cinnamon stick

½ cup *Vegetable Stock*, 17, or water

Cover and cook, stirring once or twice, over low heat until the flavors are blended, about 10 minutes.

Season with:

¼ teaspoon salt

⅛ teaspoon ground black pepper

If desired, sprinkle with:

¼ cup chopped blanched almonds, walnuts, or pecans, toasted

Bowties with Kasha (Kasha Varnishkes)

4 to 8 servings

Kasha Varnishkes is a traditional eastern European dish that is low in calories and delicious. The trick to making tender but firm, not mushy, kasha is to coat it with egg and stir it over high heat until toasted and the grains are separate. The nutty flavor of the kasha is a wonderful foil for the creamy taste of pasta. In the summer, we turn this dish into a pasta salad using whatever fresh vegetables can be found and toss with a vinaigrette dressing. Rigatoni or small shells work well here too.

Brown in a medium nonstick skillet over medium-high heat:

2 to 3 tablespoons vegetable oil

2 large onions, cut into ½-inch pieces

2 cups sliced mushrooms (button, shiitake, or portobello, or a combination), optional

1 clove garlic, minced

Salt and ground black pepper to taste

Remove to a large bowl. Cook in a large pot of boiling salted water until tender but firm:

6 ounces bowtie pasta

Drain the noodles and toss with the onion mixture. Beat in a small bowl:

1 large egg

Add:

1 cup whole kasha (whole roasted buckwheat groats)

Stir until the grains are well coated. Wipe out the skillet and heat it over high heat. Transfer the kasha mixture to the skillet and cook, stirring, until the grains are toasted and separate, 2 to 3 minutes. Reduce the heat to low and add:

2 cups hot *Vegetable Stock*, 17

Stir, cover, and simmer until the stock is absorbed and the kasha is tender but not mushy, 7 to 8 minutes. Stir in the noodle mixture. Taste and adjust the seasonings. Garnish with:

2 tablespoons chopped fresh parsley

Serve immediately. The dish can be made 1 to 2 days in advance and reheated, uncovered, in a 350°F oven. If the mixture is dry, add ¼ cup more vegetable stock.

BUCKWHEAT

The nuttiness of the kernels makes Russia's roasted buckwheat groats, or kasha, irresistible. Buy kasha, commonly sold in supermarkets, for deepest flavor, or choose unroasted groats, found in health food stores, for blander delicacy.

Baked Zucchini Stuffed with Couscous

4 servings

Preheat the oven to 400°F. Lightly oil a baking dish. Trim the stems and halve lengthwise:

2 medium zucchini

Sprinkle with:

Salt and ground black pepper to taste

Place the zucchini cut side down in the baking dish. Bake until the cut side is lightly browned, 10 to 12 minutes. Reduce the oven temperature to 350°F. Let the zucchini cool slightly. Using a teaspoon, scoop out the centers of the zucchini, leaving four ¼-inch-thick shells. Finely chop the pulp. Heat in a large skillet over medium heat:

1 tablespoon extra-virgin olive oil

Add and cook, stirring, until golden, about 5 minutes:

¼ cup chopped onions

Add the chopped zucchini along with:

⅓ cup quick-cooking, whole-wheat, or spelt couscous

1 clove garlic, finely minced

Cook, stirring, until coated with the oil. Stir in:

¾ cup *Vegetable Stock,* 17

1 tablespoon dried currants

½ teaspoon ground cinnamon

Bring to a boil. Cover and cook over low heat for 5 minutes. Uncover and let cool to room temperature. Stir in:

1 tablespoon pine nuts, toasted

Spoon the couscous mixture into the zucchini boats, dividing it evenly. Arrange in the baking dish and cover with aluminum foil. Bake until heated through, about 20 minutes. Serve hot.

Couscous with Zucchini and Cherry Tomatoes

6 servings

A good dish for summer.

Heat in a large saucepan over medium-low heat:

2 tablespoons olive oil

Add and cook, stirring, until golden, about 5 minutes:

1 medium onion, chopped

Add and cook, stirring, for 1 minute:

2 cloves garlic, minced

Stir in:

2½ cups *Vegetable Stock,* 17

1½ pounds medium zucchini, trimmed and cut into ½-inch-thick slices

Bring to a boil. Cook until the zucchini is tender but not soft, 3 to 5 minutes. Stir in:

2 tablespoons chopped fresh thyme, or 2 teaspoons dried

Stir in:

1½ cups quick-cooking couscous

1 tablespoon butter or olive oil

Remove from the heat. Cover and let stand until the stock is absorbed, about 10 minutes. Fluff the couscous with a fork. Stir in:

24 cherry tomatoes

Serve.

Winter Vegetable Couscous

10 to 12 servings

This dish is delicious with Harissa *(below left), the Moroccan chili-pepper condiment.* Ras El Hanout *(below right) is added to both the vegetables and to the couscous.*
Heat in medium skillet until moderately hot but not smoking:

¼ cup olive oil

Add and cook, stirring, until softened and just beginning to brown:

3 portobello mushrooms, wiped clean, gills removed, and thickly sliced

Remove from the heat and set aside. Heat in a large, heavy pan until moderately hot but not smoking:

¼ cup olive oil

Add:

1 red onion, quartered
1 celery root, cut into large chunks
2 white turnips, peeled and quartered
1 rutabaga, peeled and cut into 2-inch pieces

2 leeks (white and green parts), cleaned thoroughly and cut into ¼-inch-thick slices
1 medium head cauliflower, separated into florets
½ teaspoon dried thyme
½ teaspoon dried marjoram

Stir in:

1 tablespoon *Ras El Hanout, below*

Cook, covered, over medium heat until partially cooked, about 10 minutes. Stir in:

3 cups *Vegetable Stock, 17*

Continue cooking until the vegetables are tender but not overdone, 20 to 30 minutes. At the end of the cooking, the flavors of the vegetables should have blended together well, but each one should hold together and be distinct. During the last 10 minutes of cooking, stir in the reserved portobello mushrooms along with:

2 cups cooked chickpeas, rinsed and drained if canned

Season with:

Salt and ground black pepper to taste

Rinse in a sieve with tap water:

5 cups couscous

Transfer to a large saucepan and stir in:

2 tablespoons *Ras El Hanout, below*
Salt to taste

Let stand for 20 minutes, then rub the couscous through your hands to separate the grains. Ten minutes before serving, stir in:

2 cups *Vegetable Stock, 17*

Cook, covered, over medium heat to steam and heat through. To serve, mound the couscous in the center of a large platter and surround it with the vegetables. Garnish with:

10 fresh mint leaves

Harissa

About ⅓ cup

In North Africa, this fiery pepper paste is stirred into black olives, seafood stews, soups, herb salads, and vegetable dishes, or used as an ingredient in sauces for brochettes, tagines, and couscous.
Combine in a small dry skillet over medium heat and toast, shaking the pan often to prevent burning, until very aromatic, 2 to 3 minutes:

1 teaspoon caraway seeds
1 teaspoon coriander seeds
½ teaspoon cumin seeds

Remove from the heat, let cool to room temperature, and grind to a fine powder in a spice grinder, coffee grinder, or blender, or with a mortar and pestle. Add and grind again until smooth:

2 cloves garlic, quartered
Salt to taste

Add and grind until all the ingredients are well combined:

3 tablespoons sweet paprika
1 tablespoon red pepper flakes
1 tablespoon olive oil

The harissa will be very thick and dry. Transfer the paste to a small jar and cover with:

Olive oil

Store, covered, in the refrigerator; it will keep for 6 months.

Ras El Hanout

About ½ cup

Morocco's ras el hanout *contains many different elements, from seeds, leaves, flowers, roots, and bark to Spanish fly beetle, a supposed aphrodisiac.*
Mix together thoroughly:

2 tablespoons ground ginger
2 teaspoons ground black pepper
2 teaspoons ground allspice
2 teaspoons ground nutmeg
2 teaspoons ground mace
2 teaspoons ground cardamom
2 teaspoons ground cinnamon
2 teaspoons ground turmeric
1 teaspoon ground coriander
¼ teaspoon ground cloves
¼ teaspoon ground red pepper

ABOUT
EGGS

*T*he egg is nature's perfect shape. It is not surprising that so elegant a container should turn out to hold a small treasure of balanced nutrients—protein, fats, vitamins, and minerals. The egg's unique properties give it a unique versatility. Eggs bind vegetables, tenderize timbales, and provide richness to savory puddings and custards. They also give lift to ethereal main-course soufflés.

Spinach Soufflé, 124

Composition and Nutrition

The egg's shell is made of hard but slightly porous calcium carbonate and lined on the inside and outside with protective membranes. Most eggs are washed before coming to market, which removes the outside membrane or cuticle; a light coating of mineral oil is often applied to replace it. The color of the shell is an indication of the breed of the hen and has no connection with the quality of the egg or of its flavor. Brown shells are preferred by some cooks, particularly in the Northeast— and certain species of chickens lay yellow or even light pink, green, or blue eggs.

A single egg white from a large egg weighs about 1 ounce, provides about 17 calories, is almost 90 percent water, and is otherwise made up mostly of protein, with only trace amounts of vitamins and minerals. The yolk of the same egg, although smaller in size (weighing about ½ ounce), is far denser and is richer in calories (about 60), nutrients, and flavor. Besides providing fat, cholesterol, vitamins, and minerals, the yolk offers a bit of protein and a measure of lecithin—the compound with the ability to make sauces, like mayonnaise, thick and smooth. A whole egg contains all of the essential amino acids, an essential fatty acid called linoleic acid, 6 grams of protein, 4.5 grams of fat (1.5 grams of which are saturated), 213 milligrams of cholesterol, 1 gram of carbohydrate, 60 milligrams of potassium, and 65 milligrams of sodium, as well as 13 vitamins— almost all except C and niacin.

Americans have been eating far fewer eggs in the last twenty years, in large part because of concern over cholesterol, which is found in ample supply in egg yolks. (Egg whites contain no cholesterol.) Recent studies, however, suggest that eating eggs in moderation has little effect on the level of blood cholesterol, and most nutritionists agree that eggs have a place in a well-rounded, well-balanced diet. If cholesterol is a concern, see *Making Egg Substitutes, opposite.*

Quality, Safety, and Storing

The quality of an egg is largely a matter of how old it is; the best eggs are the freshest. Age is not the only determining factor, however. The shell naturally protects an egg, and if it is cracked or damaged, the contents will deteriorate rapidly; eggs with cracked, damaged, or dirty shells should not be used. Also important are the variables of temperature (eggs should be stored at less than 40°F), humidity (the ideal range is 70 to 80 percent), and handling (which means prompt and frequent gathering, along with washing and oiling of the shell by the producer). A week-old egg, properly stored, can be fresher than an egg left at room temperature for just one day. Look for the date or freshness code required on the carton of any USDA-inspected eggs. Always buy eggs from a refrigerated case rather than a room-temperature display.

Fresh eggs, if refrigerated without interruption, should retain their quality for at least 1 month, although the whites will become noticeably thinner. Because they are repeatedly exposed to warm air, eggs stored in those handy slots in the refrigerator door will deteriorate more quickly than those kept in their carton, set on an inside shelf.

If you are unsure of the age of your eggs, just before using them, place them in a bowl of cold water. Those that float—a sign that the egg inside has shrunk through extended moisture loss—are not usable. You can also break an egg into a clean bowl and smell it. An old or stale egg will smell like damp grass or straw and will taint any delicate or pure egg dishes.

The bacteria *Salmonella enteritidis,* which can cause illness and even death, is occasionally found in raw eggs, even uncracked eggs. While the risk remains extremely low (even infected eggs may not cause problems if properly stored and cooked), we recommend handling eggs carefully, particularly when cooking for young children, the elderly, pregnant women, or anyone with a compromised immune system.

HOW TO SEPARATE EGGS

Separating eggs can be done with an egg separator or by hand.

1 To use an egg separator, place the device on the rim of a cup or small bowl. Crack the egg carefully into the center. The white will run through the slits around the sides into the container below, while the yolk will sit in the depression of the separator.

2 To separate by hand, have three bowls ready. Holding an egg in one hand, tap the egg on the edge of one of the bowls to make an even, crosswise break. Holding the egg over a bowl, pull the edges apart until the eggshell is broken into halves. Some of the egg white will immediately flow into the bowl.

3 Pour the remaining egg back and forth from one half-shell to the other, letting more of the white flow into the bowl each time until only the yolk remains in the shell. During this shifting process, you will be able to tell quickly if there is any discoloration or off odor, in which case you should discard the entire egg immediately. Should the yolk break during this process, you can try to remove any yolk particles from the white with the corner of a paper towel moistened with cold water. If this fails, the white may still be used for anything other than beaten egg whites; even the smallest speck of yolk can prevent egg whites from frothing. If the white is fresh and speckless, transfer it to the second bowl and the yolk to the third.

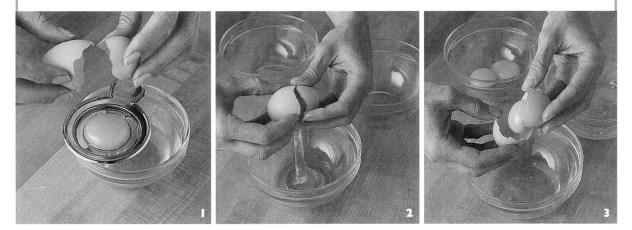

MAKING EGG SUBSTITUTES

Most egg-replacement products are 98 to 99 percent egg whites and thus lack the yolk-rich taste of whole eggs. Egg whites are also apt to dry out when cooked. You can make your own egg substitute by gently mixing together 12 egg whites, 1 tablespoon vegetable oil, and ¼ teaspoon salt. About ⅓ cup of this mixture is the equivalent volume of a whole egg. You can also substitute egg whites for up to half of the whole eggs in a recipe. Figure 1½ egg whites (or a scant 3 tablespoons) for every whole egg you omit.

EGG GRADES AND SIZES

Most eggs sold in the supermarkets are labeled either grade AA or grade A. These are the top two classifications of the USDA's voluntary system for indicating an egg's quality before it is shipped to the marketplace. These grades have no bearing on size or freshness. Rather, both AA and A indicate eggs that had high, round yolks and firm, thick whites when they were first laid. While eggs graded AA are a bit more shapely, the difference between the two grades is slight, and in time, no matter what its grade, any egg yolk will flatten out and the white will turn watery. The most common egg size sold today is large, and our recipes, unless they state otherwise, use large eggs.

Sometimes it is convenient or necessary to weigh or measure eggs out of the shell. Any time you need only part of an egg, beat the egg slightly to make it easier to measure. Use the following conversions:

**1 large egg white = 1 ounce =
  2 tablespoons**
**1 large egg yolk = ½ ounce =
  1 tablespoon**

Asparagus Frittata

4 servings

A frittata is the Italian version of an omelet. It is more robust than the classic French omelet and a bit easier to handle. Instead of trying to flip the frittata, we recommend popping it under the broiler to cook the top side. Served in wedges, frittatas are delicious hot, warm, or at room temperature.

Heat in a large skillet over medium heat:

2 tablespoons olive oil

Add and cook until lightly browned, about 10 minutes:

¾ to 1 cup lightly steamed asparagus tips and pieces

Season with:

¼ teaspoon salt
⅛ teaspoon ground black pepper

Transfer the asparagus to a strainer to drain off the excess oil. Let cool completely.

Preheat the broiler.

Meanwhile, beat together until smooth:

5 eggs
½ teaspoon salt
Pinch of ground black pepper

Add the cooled asparagus along with:

½ cup grated Parmesan cheese (optional)
1 tablespoon minced fresh parsley

Heat in a large, ovenproof skillet over medium heat:

2 tablespoons olive oil or butter

When hot, pour in the egg mixture.

Reduce the heat and cook until the bottom is set, then place under the broiler for 30 to 60 seconds to finish cooking. A traditional frittata is not browned. Loosen the frittata with a spatula and slide it onto a plate. Cut into wedges.

ZUCCHINI FRITTATA

Prepare *Asparagus Frittata, above,* substituting 3 medium zucchini, sliced, and 1 cup thinly sliced onions for the asparagus. Add 1 tablespoon finely shredded fresh basil with the Parmesan cheese and parsley.

Artichoke Frittata

8 servings

Cut off the stem and top two-thirds of:

6 medium artichokes

Place the artichokes bottom side up on the work surface and cut away the dark green outer leaves with quick, short strokes, beginning at the stem and working out. Once the white flesh is exposed, trim off all the remaining leaves. Scoop out the center choke area with a grapefruit spoon or teaspoon and cut the artichoke bottom into 8 pieces.

Melt in a large, well-seasoned cast-iron skillet over medium heat:

3 tablespoons unsalted butter

Add and cook, stirring, until softened but not browned, about

5 minutes:

2 medium leeks, cleaned thoroughly and chopped
1 large clove garlic, chopped

Add the artichoke pieces along with:

¾ cup water
1 tablespoon fresh lemon juice

Cover and simmer over medium-low heat until the artichoke hearts are just tender, 12 to 15 minutes. Add more water if needed. Meanwhile roast, 58, peel, seed, and thinly slice:

1 red bell pepper

Whisk together:

12 large eggs
1¼ cups half-and-half
1 cup grated Parmesan cheese
½ cup chopped fresh basil

1 teaspoon salt
Ground black pepper to taste

Preheat the broiler.

When the artichokes are just tender, remove the lid and cook until the liquid is evaporated. Add:

2 tablespoons butter

Swirl to melt and coat the pan. Give the egg mixture a quick whisking and add to the pan. Stir in the roasted peppers. Cook the frittata over medium-low heat until the center is almost set, about 18 minutes. If desired, cook the frittata under the broiler until browned, about 2 minutes. Cool to warm and serve from the skillet in thin slices.

Huevos Rancheros

4 servings

In this classic Mexican dish, fried eggs are placed on a tortilla, then smothered with a spicy, rustic tomato chili pepper sauce. Typically, these eggs are accompanied with Refried Beans, 81.

Prepare and keep warm:

2 cups *Roasted Tomato–Chipotle Salsa,* right

In a large, nonstick skillet, heat over medium-high heat:

1 to 2 tablespoons vegetable oil

When hot, add 1 at a time and quick-fry for 2 to 3 seconds each side:

4 corn tortillas

Remove to paper towels to drain, then wrap in foil and keep warm in a 200°F oven. Set the skillet over medium-low heat (or use two skillets if the eggs will not all fit at once) and add a bit more oil if needed. Break into the skillet:

4 to 8 eggs

Let cook until set, sunny-side-up. Cover the pan for a minute or so for the most even cooking. Season with:

Salt and ground black pepper to taste

Set a tortilla on each of 4 warmed plates and top with 1 or 2 eggs. Spoon a generous ½ cup of the warm tomato-chipotle sauce around each serving. Serve immediately sprinkled with:

Finely crumbled Mexican queso fresco, farmer's cheese, or feta cheese

Chopped fresh cilantro

Roasted Tomato–Chipotle Salsa

About 2 cups

Tomatoes—and the salsa they create—take on a deeper flavor when roasted. Chipotle peppers (dried smoked jalapeños) have made great gains in popularity in this country for their intense, rich, smoky flavor. They show up everywhere, from salsas and canned tomato sauce (adobo) to stews, soups, and more.

Build a medium-low fire in your grill or preheat the broiler.

Place on the grill or on a broiler pan:

6 medium, ripe tomatoes, seeded, if desired, and halved

Grill or broil (broil as close to the heat as possible), turning as needed, until the skins are blackened in spots and slightly softened, about 5 minutes each side on the grill and slightly less time in the broiler. When cool enough to handle, remove the skins and coarsely chop the tomatoes, put them in a medium bowl, and stir in:

1 small onion, finely chopped, rinsed, and drained

¼ cup coarsely chopped fresh cilantro

3 tablespoons fresh lime juice, or to taste

2 tablespoons olive oil

2 cloves garlic, finely chopped

1½ teaspoons finely chopped canned chipotle pepper, or to taste

1 teaspoon ground cumin

Salt to taste

Serve immediately.

Vegetable Timbale

4 servings

Timbale is the French word for "kettle drum" and refers to any savory custard baked in a small, high-sided, tapered drum-shaped mold. In its modern usage, a timbale is any savory custard cooked in an individual mold and then inverted and unmolded before serving.

Position a rack in the lower third of the oven. Preheat the oven to 325°F. Lightly grease four 6-ounce ramekins or custard cups.

Steam or blanch until crisp-tender:

2 cups coarsely chopped cauliflower florets, broccoli florets, or zucchini or 2 cups corn kernels

Drain thoroughly and either finely chop or pulse in a food processor. Transfer to a bowl. Melt in a small skillet over medium heat:

1 tablespoon unsalted butter

Add and cook, stirring, until softened, 2 to 3 minutes:

¼ cup minced shallots (about 2)

Add to the vegetables and season with:

2 tablespoons Madeira (optional)
½ teaspoon salt
⅛ teaspoon freshly grated or ground nutmeg
Ground black pepper to taste

Heat almost to a boil:

1 cup light or heavy cream

Whisk into the vegetables:

3 large eggs

Slowly whisk in the hot cream and ladle the custard into the prepared dishes. Sprinkle the tops with:

¼ cup grated Parmesan cheese (optional)

Place the dishes in a water bath (opposite). Cover the pan with aluminum foil and bake until the custard is set two-thirds of the way to the center of the dishes, 25 to 30 minutes. Remove from the oven, loosen the cover but leave it on, and return to the oven to cook for another 10 minutes. Let cool for 10 minutes, then run a knife around the inside edge of the ramekins. Invert the timbales onto serving plates. Serve sprinkled with:

Chopped fresh parsley or snipped fresh chives (optional)

Corn Pudding with Roasted Poblano Peppers

6 servings

Position a rack in the center of the oven. Butter a 1½-quart gratin or soufflé dish.
Roast, 58:

3 poblano or New Mexico green chili peppers

Peel, remove the seeds and veins, then chop.
Cut and scrape the kernels from:

4 ears sweet corn (about 2 cups)

Heat in a large skillet over medium heat:

2 tablespoons butter or corn oil

Add and cook for 5 minutes:

1 onion, diced
2 teaspoons minced garlic

½ teaspoon dried oregano

Stir in the corn kernels and roasted peppers. Cook for 3 minutes, then let cool. Combine in another bowl:

4 large eggs, lightly beaten
¾ cup grated Monterey Jack or Muenster cheese
½ cup grated sharp Cheddar cheese
Salt and ground black pepper to taste

Add the cooled corn mixture and scrape into the prepared dish. Bake until puffed and golden, about 30 minutes.

Spoon Bread

6 to 8 servings

This corn bread is soft enough to eat with a spoon or fork. For a light meal, sprinkle with grated cheese or add a dollop of sour cream and spicy salsa on the side and serve with a green salad.

Position a rack in the center of the oven. Preheat the oven to 375°F. Grease an 8 x 8-inch baking dish.
In a large, heavy saucepan, bring to a simmer:

2½ cups milk
2 tablespoons unsalted butter
1 teaspoon salt

Reduce the heat to low. Add in a slow, steady stream, whisking constantly to prevent lumps:

1 cup cornmeal

Increase the heat to medium and cook, stirring constantly, until the mixture is thick and shiny, 3 to 4 minutes. Remove from the heat and set aside to cool for 3 to 4 minutes. Whisk together:

3 large egg yolks
½ cup cream or milk

Stir gradually into the cornmeal mixture. Beat on medium speed until the peaks are stiff but not dry:

3 large egg whites
⅛ teaspoon cream of tartar (optional)

Fold one-quarter of the egg whites into the cornmeal mixture to lighten it, then fold in the remaining whites. Scrape the batter into the baking dish and spread evenly. Bake until the bread has risen like a soufflé, with a golden brown surface, and a knife inserted in the center comes out clean, 25 to 35 minutes. Serve immediately.

THE WATER BATH

By baking a dish of custard in a larger pan of water, also known as the bain-marie or "Maria's bath," the cook partially insulates the custard from the oven's heat and thereby protects it from overcooking. All you need is a roasting pan large enough to accommodate the custards comfortably. Set a cake rack in the pan or cover the pan bottom with a dish towel or several layers of paper towels so the custards will not be in direct contact with the hot pan bottom. Arrange the custards in the dry pan, slip the pan into a preheated oven, and immediately pour enough scalding-hot tap water into the pan to come one-half to two-thirds of the way up the sides of the custard dishes.

Tomato and Goat Cheese Quiche

One 9-inch quiche; 6 servings

The most famous of savory custards is quiche, a custard containing small bits of vegetables and/or cheese baked in a tart or pie crust. The basic proportions are 3 to 4 whole eggs for every 2 cups of milk. Using cream in place of milk or replacing one whole egg with 2 yolks gives you a richer, more custardy quiche. Quiche is traditionally prepared in a prebaked tart shell brushed with egg yolk to help prevent it from becoming soggy. Tomato and goat cheese make an excellent quiche, but fillings are endlessly variable.

Prepare:

½ recipe *Flaky Pastry Dough, below*

Roll out the dough ⅛ inch thick and fit into a buttered 9-inch quiche, tart, or pie pan. Refrigerate while you prepare the filling.

Set a rack in the lowest position in the oven. Preheat the oven to 400°F.

Prepare and set aside:

1 pound plum tomatoes (about 6), cored, quartered lengthwise, and seeded

Crumble into a bowl:

4 ounces fresh goat cheese

Slowly mash in with the back of a wooden spoon until smooth:

¾ cup half-and-half or heavy cream

½ cup milk

Add and whisk until smooth:

3 large eggs

1 tablespoon chopped fresh parsley

1½ teaspoons chopped fresh thyme or savory or 3 tablespoons chopped fresh basil

¼ teaspoon salt

Plenty of ground black pepper

Remove the pastry shell from the refrigerator and arrange the tomato quarters in the shell like the spokes of a wheel, with the pointed end (blossom end) toward the center of the quiche. Fill in the center with more tomato quarters. Pour the cheese mixture over the tomatoes and bake until the pastry and top are golden brown, 40 to 45 minutes. Let the quiche rest for 10 minutes to settle, then cut into wedges and serve.

Flaky Pastry Dough

Two 9-inch pie crusts, or two 9½- or 10-inch tart crusts, or one 9-inch covered pie crust

This dough makes a light, flaky crust that shatters at the touch of a fork. If you need only a single pie or tart crust, decrease all ingredients by half or freeze half the dough for future use.

Using a rubber spatula, thoroughly mix in a large bowl:

2½ cups all-purpose flour

1 teaspoon white sugar or 1 tablespoon powdered sugar

1 teaspoon salt

Add:

1 cup solid vegetable shortening, or ½ cup shortening and 8 tablespoons (1 stick) cold unsalted butter

Break the shortening into large chunks; if using butter, cut it into small pieces, then add it to the flour mixture. Cut the fat into the dry ingredients by chopping vigorously with a pastry blender or by cutting in opposite directions with 2 knives, one held in each hand. As you work, periodically stir dry flour up from the bottom of the bowl and scrape clinging fat off the pastry blender or knives. When you are through, some of the fat should remain in pea-sized pieces; the rest should be reduced to the consistency of coarse crumbs or cornmeal. The mixture should seem dry and powdery and not pasty or greasy. Drizzle over the flour and fat mixture:

⅓ cup plus 1 tablespoon ice water

Using the rubber spatula, cut with the blade side until the mixture looks evenly moistened and begins to form small balls. Press down on the dough with the flat side of the spatula. If the balls of dough stick together, you have added enough water; if they do not, drizzle over the top:

1 to 2 tablespoons ice water

Cut in the water, again using the blade of the spatula, then press with your hands until the dough coheres. The dough should look rough, not smooth. Divide the dough in half, press each half into a round flat disk, and wrap tightly in plastic. Refrigerate for at least 30 minutes, and preferably for several hours, or for up to 2 days before rolling. The dough can also be wrapped airtight and frozen for up to 6 months; thaw completely before rolling.

Spinach Soufflé

6 servings

Preheat the oven to 375°F. Generously butter an 8-cup soufflé dish or six 8-ounce ramekins and dust the insides with:

¼ to ½ cup dry breadcrumbs or grated Parmesan cheese

Shake out the excess. Combine in a bowl or large saucepan:

1½ cups *Thick Béchamel Sauce, opposite*, at room temperature or slightly warmed

¾ teaspoon salt

⅛ teaspoon ground nutmeg or red pepper

Pinch of ground white pepper

Beat ½ cup of the mixture into:

6 large egg yolks

¾ cup grated Parmesan or Swiss cheese, or a combination

Combine with the rest of the sauce, beating vigorously to blend. Add:

1½ cups cooked spinach, squeezed dry and finely chopped

Beat until stiff but not dry:

6 large egg whites

Pinch of salt

Stir one-quarter of the whites into the soufflé base to lighten it, then fold in the rest. Pour into the prepared soufflé dish or ramekins. Bake until the soufflé is risen and golden brown on top, 40 to 45 minutes (20 to 25 minutes for individual soufflés). Remove from the oven and serve immediately.

CARROT SOUFFLÉ

Prepare *Spinach Soufflé, left*, substituting pureed cooked carrots for the spinach. Add 1 tablespoon minced fresh thyme or dill to the base.

MUSHROOM SOUFFLÉ

Prepare *Spinach Soufflé, left*, substituting sautéed finely chopped mushrooms (preferably cremini) for the spinach. If desired, ½ to 1 cup grated Gruyère cheese can be substituted for the Parmesan. For additional herbs, try 1½ teaspoons chopped fresh marjoram or rosemary.

Make-Ahead Goat Cheese and Walnut Soufflés

8 servings

These are more substantial than traditional soufflés, but they are wonderful in their own right. Serve them on a lightly dressed bed of field greens.

Preheat the oven to 350°F. Combine:

¾ cup walnuts, toasted and finely chopped

¼ cup cornmeal

Generously butter eight 6-ounce ramekins or custard cups and sprinkle the insides with the cornmeal mixture, tilting in all directions until completely coated. Scatter any nuts that do not adhere over the bottoms of the dishes.

Melt in a saucepan over medium heat:

3 tablespoons unsalted butter

Stir in until smooth:

¼ cup all-purpose flour

Cook, stirring, for 1 minute. Remove from the heat and stir in:

⅔ cup milk

Return to the heat and, stirring very briskly, bring to a boil. (The mixture will be very thick.) Scrape into a bowl. Add and mash until the cheese is melted:

10 ounces fresh unripened goat cheese

Beat in:

4 large egg yolks

2 cloves garlic, very finely minced

¼ teaspoon dried thyme

¼ teaspoon salt

¼ teaspoon ground white pepper

Beat until stiff but not dry:

5 large egg whites

¼ teaspoon cream of tartar

Stir one-quarter of the whites into the soufflé base to lighten it, then fold in the rest. Pour into the prepared ramekins and smooth the tops. Place the ramekins in a water bath, 121. Bake until a skewer inserted in the center comes out almost clean, about 30 minutes. Let stand for 15 minutes in the water bath, then invert the ramekins onto a greased baking sheet. The soufflés can be served immediately or cooled, covered tightly with plastic wrap, and refrigerated for up to 3 days. When ready to serve, heat the soufflés in a 425°F oven until warmed through, 5 to 7 minutes.

Sauce Béchamel (White Sauce)

About 1 cup

Combine in a small saucepan over very low heat:

1¼ cups milk

¼ onion with 1 bay leaf stuck to it using 2 whole cloves

Pinch of freshly grated nutmeg (optional)

Simmer gently for 15 minutes, uncovered, to infuse flavor into the milk. Discard the onion, bay leaf, and cloves. Meanwhile, melt in a medium, heavy saucepan over low heat:

2 tablespoons unsalted butter

Stir in:

2 tablespoons all-purpose flour

Cook, uncovered, stirring occasionally with a wooden spoon or spatula, over medium-low heat until the roux is just fragrant but not darkened, 2 to 3 minutes. Remove from the heat and let cool slightly. Slowly whisk in the warm milk and return the saucepan to the heat. Bring the sauce slowly to a simmer, whisking to prevent lumps. Cook, stirring often and skimming any skin that forms on the surface, over low heat, without boiling, until it reaches the consistency of thick cream soup, 8 to 10 minutes. Strain through a fine-mesh sieve, if desired. Season with:

Salt and ground white pepper to taste

THIN BÉCHAMEL SAUCE

Use as a quick base for cream soups.
Prepare *Sauce Béchamel, above,* decreasing the butter to 1 tablespoon and the flour to 1 tablespoon. The finished sauce should be thick enough to coat the back of a spoon.

THICK BÉCHAMEL SAUCE

Use as a soufflé base or to bind a runny casserole.
Prepare *Sauce Béchamel, above,* increasing the butter to 3 tablespoons and the flour to 3 tablespoons.

Index

Bold type indicates that a recipe has
an accompanying photograph.

ACKNOWLEDGMENTS

Special thanks to my wife and editor in residence, Susan; our indispensable assistant and comrade, Mary Gilbert; and our friends and agents, Gene Winick and Sam Pinkus. Much appreciation also goes to Simon & Schuster, Scribner, and Weldon Owen for their devotion to this project. Thank you Carolyn, Susan, Bill, Marah, John, Terry, Roger, Gaye, Val, Norman, and all the other capable and talented folks who gave a part of themselves to the Joy of Cooking All About series.

My eternal appreciation goes to the food experts, writers, and editors whose contributions and collaborations are at the heart of Joy—especially Stephen Schmidt. He was to the 1997 edition what Chef Pierre Adrian was to Mom's final editions of Joy. Thank you one and all.

Ethan Becker

FOOD EXPERTS, WRITERS, AND EDITORS

Selma Abrams, Jody Adams, Samia Ahad, Bruce Aidells, Katherine Alford, Deirdre Allen, Pam Anderson, Elizabeth Andoh, Phillip Andres, Alice Arndt, John Ash, Nancy Baggett, Rick and Deann Bayless, Lee E. Benning, Rose Levy Beranbaum, Brigit Legere Binns, Jack Bishop, Carole Bloom, Arthur Boehm, Ed Brown, JeanMarie Brownson, Larry Catanzaro, Val Cipollone, Polly Clingerman, Elaine Corn, Bruce Cost, Amy Cotler, Brian Crawley, Gail Damerow, Linda Dann, Deirdre Davis, Jane Spencer Davis, Erica De Mane, Susan Derecskey, Abigail Johnson Dodge, Jim Dodge, Aurora Esther, Michele Fagerroos, Eva Forson, Margaret Fox, Betty Fussell, Mary Gilbert, Darra Goldstein, Elaine Gonzalez, Dorie Greenspan, Maria Guarnaschelli, Helen Gustafson, Pat Haley, Gordon Hamersley, Melissa Hamilton, Jessica Harris, Hallie Harron, Nao Hauser, William Hay, Larry Hayden, Kate Hays, Marcella Hazan, Tim Healea, Janie Hibler, Lee Hofstetter, Paula Hogan, Rosemary Howe, Mike Hughes, Jennifer Humphries, Dana Jacobi, Stephen Johnson, Lynne Rossetto Kasper, Denis Kelly, Fran Kennedy, Johanne Killeen and George Germon, Shirley King, Maya Klein, Diane M. Kochilas, Phyllis Kohn, Aglaia Kremezi, Mildred Kroll, Loni Kuhn, Corby Kummer, Virginia Lawrence, Jill Leigh, Karen Levin, Lori Longbotham, Susan Hermann Loomis, Emily Luchetti, Stephanie Lyness, Karen MacNeil, Deborah Madison, Linda Marino, Kathleen McAndrews, Alice Medrich, Anne Mendelson, Lisa Montenegro, Cindy Mushet, Marion Nestle, Toby Oksman, Joyce O'Neill, Suzen O'Rourke, Russ Parsons, Holly Pearson, James Peterson, Marina Petrakos, Mary Placek, Maricel Presilla, Marion K. Pruitt, Adam Rapoport, Mardee Haidin Regan, Peter Reinhart, Sarah Anne Reynolds, Madge Rosenberg, Nicole Routhier, Jon Rowley, Nancy Ross Ryan, Chris Schlesinger, Stephen Schmidt, Lisa Schumacher, Marie Simmons, Nina Simonds, A. Cort Sinnes, Sue Spitler, Marah Stets, Molly Stevens, Christopher Stoye, Susan Stuck, Sylvia Thompson, Jean and Pierre Troisgros, Jill Van Cleave, Patricia Wells, Laurie Wenk, Caroline Wheaton, Jasper White, Jonathan White, Marilyn Wilkenson, Carla Williams, Virginia Willis, John Willoughby, Deborah Winson, Lisa Yockelson.

Weldon Owen wishes to thank the following people and organizations for their generous assistance and support in producing this book: Desne Border, Ken DellaPenta, Oldways Preservation & Exchange Trust, and Joan Olson.